宣　公　上　人　德　相

慈悲普度信者得救成正覺

過化存神禮之獲福悟無生

The Venerable Master Hsuan Hua

His kindness and compassion cross over all; Believers are liberated and perfect the Right Enlightenment.

Transforming beings wherever he goes, his spirit remains intact;

Those who venerate him obtain blessings and awaken to the Unproduced.

Medicine Master Sutra

Sutra of the Merit and Virtue of the Past Vows of Medicine Master Vaiḍūrya Light Tathāgata

English translation by the
Buddhist Text Translation Society

Buddhist Text Translation Society
Dharma Realm Buddhist University
Dharma Realm Buddhist Association
Burlingame, California U.S.A.

Sutra of the Merit and Virtue of the Past Vows
of Medicine Master Vaiḍūrya Light Tathāgata

Published and translated by:

Buddhist Text Translation Society
1777 Murchison Drive, Burlingame, CA 94010-4504

©1997 Buddhist Text Translation Society
Dharma Realm Buddhist University
Dharma Realm Buddhist Association

First Chinese edition published 1996 as
藥師琉璃光如來本願功德經淺釋
(yao shi liu li guang ru lai ben yuan gong de jing qian shi)

First English edition published 1997

06 05 04 03 02 01 00 99 98 97   10 9 8 7 6 5 4 3 2 1

Printed in Malaysia

Pinyin is used for the romanization of Chinese words,
except for proper names which retain familiar romanizations.

Library of Congress Cataloging-in-Publication Data

Hsüan Hua, 1908 –
    [Yao shih liu li kuang pen yuen kung te ching ch'ien shih. English]
    Sutra of the merit and virtue of the past vows of Medicine Master
Vaidurya Light Tathagata : a simple explanation / by the Ven. Master
Hsuan Hua ; English translation by the Buddhist Text Translation
Society. — 1st English ed.
        p.   cm.
    Includes index.
    ISBN 0-88139-306-1 (hc : alk. paper)
    1. Tripiṭaka. Sūtrapiṭaka. Bhaiṣajyaguruvaidūryaprabharājasūtra-
–Commentaries.
BQ2240.B537H7813   1997
294.3'85 — dc21   97–409
                                                        CIP

Contents

The Eight Guidelines of
The Buddhist Text Translation Society

1. A volunteer must free him/herself from the motives of personal fame and profit.

2. A volunteer must cultivate a respectful and sincere attitude free from arrogance and conceit.

3. A volunteer must refrain from aggrandizing his/her work and denigrating that of others.

4. A volunteer must not establish him/herself as the standard of correctness and suppress the work of others with his or her fault-finding.

5. A volunteer must take the Buddha-mind as his/her own mind.

6. A volunteer must use the wisdom of Dharma-Selecting Vision to determine true principles.

7. A volunteer must request Virtuous Elders in the ten directions to certify his/her translations.

8. A volunteer must endeavor to propagate the teachings by printing Sutras, Shastra texts, and Vinaya texts when the translations are certified as being correct.

Preface

Seeing that living beings in the world have contracted serious illnesses and are undergoing tremendous suffering, the Buddhas, the Bodhisattvas, Those Enlightened to Conditions, and the Hearers come to their aid by propagating the Buddhadharma to rescue them. Basically, there is no difference between the Buddhas and living beings. Those who fall ill are living beings, and those who prescribe medicine and alleviate suffering are Buddhas. They are like parents and child. When the child is sick, the parents also fall ill. When the child is well, they also recover. Thus the Buddha says, "I am sick because living beings are ill. I am well when living beings are well."

The Buddha speaks limitless Dharmas, which are like medicines, to alleviate the illnesses of living beings. All Tathagatas are skilled in curing the afflictions and sicknesses of living beings. They are known as great physicians. Based on his compassionate vow to quell disasters and lengthen life, Medicine Master Buddha has established the Vaidurya Pure Land in the East, and he is the Teaching Host there. The name "Medicine Master" illustrates his virtue in prescribing medicines expediently in order to alleviate the myriad sicknesses. He is honored as the foremost teacher in medicine, the king of medicine kings. Shakyamuni Buddha, out of compassion for living beings who are suffering for their offenses, expounded the twelve great vows that Medicine Master Buddha made in the causal stage of cultivation.

Where does the multitude of illnesses and sufferings come from? All dharmas arise from the mind alone, and so, too, do all illnesses. As long as one is engaged in fighting, greed, seeking, selfishness, wanting personal advantage, lying, scheming, begging, and asking for things, these are sources of illness. Hence over the past few decades the Venerable Master Hua has emphasized the three guidelines: "Freezing, we do not scheme; starving, we do not beg; dying of poverty, we ask for nothing," and the six principles: no fighting, no greed, no seeking, no selfishness, no wanting personal advantage, and no lying. These pure precepts, which coincide with the mind of the Buddhas above and suit the faculties of living beings below, are like the wonderful agada medicine which cures all illnesses. One who can abide by these principles will definitely attain Buddhahood. Moreover, he will also be propagating the Medicine Master Dharma-door and actualizing the Vaidurya Pure Land.

Over the past decades, the Buddhist Text Translation Society of the Dharma Realm Buddhist Association has been translating Buddhist texts into the various languages of the world, with the hope that all living beings will be able to benefit from the limitless wonderful medicines of the greatly compassionate World Honored One. With the publication of this English volume of the *Sutra of the Merit and Virtue of the Past Vows of Medicine Master Vaidurya Light Tathagata* with the Venerable Master Hua's brief and yet profound explanation, we hope that living beings will all take this wondrous medicine so that they can relieve their sufferings and attain the Buddha Way together.

Bhikshuni Heng Tung
June 1997

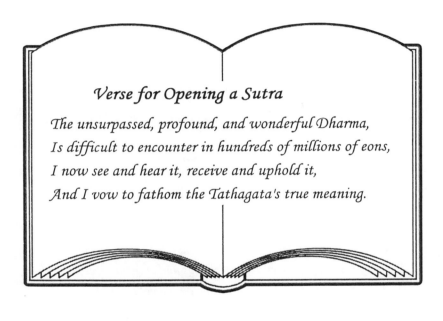

Verse for Opening a Sutra

The unsurpassed, profound, and wonderful Dharma,
Is difficult to encounter in hundreds of millions of eons,
I now see and hear it, receive and uphold it,
And I vow to fathom the Tathagata's true meaning.

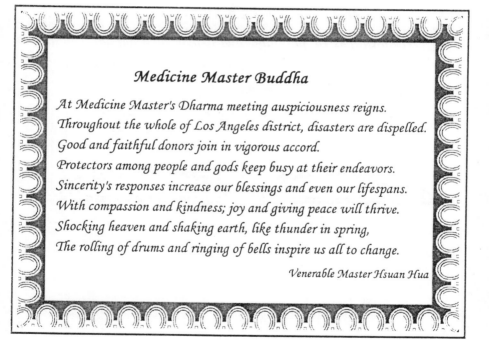

Medicine Master Buddha

At Medicine Master's Dharma meeting auspiciousness reigns.
Throughout the whole of Los Angeles district, disasters are dispelled.
Good and faithful donors join in vigorous accord.
Protectors among people and gods keep busy at their endeavors.
Sincerity's responses increase our blessings and even our lifespans.
With compassion and kindness; joy and giving peace will thrive.
Shocking heaven and shaking earth, like thunder in spring,
The rolling of drums and ringing of bells inspire us all to change.

Venerable Master Hsuan Hua

Sutra of the Merit and Virtue of the Past Vows of Medicine Master Vaiḍūrya Light Tathāgata

SUTRA:

Thus I have heard. At one time the Bhagavan was travelling through various lands to teach living beings. He arrived at Vaiśālī [*"City of Extensive Adornments"*] and stayed beneath a tree from which music resounded. With him were eight thousand great Bhikshus and thirty-six thousand Bodhisattvas Mahāsattvas; also kings, ministers, Brahmans, lay disciples; gods, dragons, and the rest of the eightfold division; beings both human and non-human. The immeasurable great multitude respectfully surrounded him, and he spoke Dharma for them.

At that time, the Dharma Prince Mañjuśrī, receiving the awesome inspiration of the Buddha, rose from his seat, bared one of his shoulders, knelt on his right knee, and, inclining his head and placing his palms together, said to the Bhagavan, "World Honored One! We wish you would speak about such Dharmas as the Buddhas' names, the great vows they made in the past, and their supreme merit and virtue, so that those who hear them will be rid of their karmic hindrances. This request is also for the sake of bringing benefit and joy to sentient beings in the Dharma-Image Age."

The Buddha then praised the Pure Youth Mañjuśrī: "Good indeed! Good indeed, Mañjuśrī. With great compassion you now request that I speak about the Buddhas' names and the merit and virtue of their past vows, for the sake of rescuing sentient beings who are bound up by karmic obstacles, and for the purpose of bringing benefit, peace, and joy to beings who live in the Dharma-Image Age. Listen attentively to my words and reflect on them extremely well, for I will now answer you."

Mañjuśrī said, "Please do speak. We are glad to listen."

The Buddha told Mañjuśrī, "Passing from here to the east, beyond Buddhalands numerous as the sand grains in ten Ganges rivers, is a world called 'Pure Vaiḍūrya.' The Buddha there is named Medicine Master Vaiḍūrya Light Tathāgata, Of Proper and Equal Enlightenment, Perfect in Understanding and Practice, Well Gone One, One Who Understands the World, Supreme Lord, Regulating Hero, Teacher of Gods and Humans, Buddha, Bhagavan. Mañjuśrī, when that World Honored One, Medicine Master Vaiḍūrya Light Tathāgata, was practicing the Bodhisattva path in the past, he made twelve great vows that enable all sentient beings to obtain what they seek.

"The first great vow: 'I vow that in a future life, when I attain *anuttarasamyaksambodhi*, my body will shine with dazzling light that will illumine measureless, countless, boundless worlds. My body will be adorned with the thirty-two heroic features and the eighty subsidiary characteristics, and I will enable all beings to become as I am.'

"The second great vow: 'I vow that in a future life when I attain Bodhi, my body will be as bright and clear

2

as *vaiḍūrya*, flawlessly pure, vastly radiant, majestic with merit and virtue, abiding at ease, adorned with blazing nets brighter than the sun and the moon. Beings dwelling in darkness will be illuminated and will succeed in all their endeavors.'

"The third great vow: 'I vow that in a future life when I attain Bodhi, I will, by means of limitless, unbounded wisdom and skill-in-means, enable all sentient beings to obtain an inexhaustible supply of material necessities so they are without the slightest want.'

"The fourth great vow: 'I vow that in a future life when I attain Bodhi, I shall lead those sentient beings who practice deviant paths to reside in the Way of Bodhi, and those who travel on the vehicles of the Hearer or Pratyekabuddha to abide in the Great Vehicle.'

"The fifth great vow: 'I vow that in a future life when I attain Bodhi, I shall enable limitless and boundless numbers of sentient beings who cultivate Brahma conduct within my Dharma to perfectly uphold the three clusters of precepts without exception. Should there be any violation, upon hearing my name, they will regain their purity and not fall into the evil destinies.'

"The sixth great vow: 'I vow that in a future life when I attain Bodhi, if there are sentient beings whose bodies are inferior and whose faculties are imperfect, who are ugly, dull, blind, deaf, mute, deformed, paralyzed, hunch-backed, or afflicted with skin disease, insanity, or various other sicknesses and sufferings, upon hearing my name they shall all become endowed with upright features, keen intelligence, and perfect faculties, and they shall be free of sickness and suffering.'

"The seventh great vow: 'I vow that in a future life when I attain Bodhi, I shall cause sentient beings who are oppressed by many illnesses and who are without aid, without a place to turn, without a doctor, without medicine, without relatives, and without a family, who are poverty-stricken and filled with suffering to be cured of their sicknesses upon having my name pass by their ear, so they are peaceful and happy in body and mind. They will have a family and relatives, and acquire an abundance of property and wealth, and even realize unsurpassed Bodhi.'

"The eighth great vow: 'I vow that in a future life when I attain Bodhi, if there are women who give rise to a deep loathing for their female body and wish to renounce it because they are oppressed and disturbed by the myriad sufferings of being female, upon hearing my name, they will be able to turn from women into men who are replete with male features and ultimately realize unsurpassed Bodhi.'

"The ninth great vow: 'I vow that in a future life when I attain Bodhi, I shall liberate sentient beings from the nets of demons and the bonds of external sects. If they have fallen into the dense forests of evil views, I shall lead them to have proper views and to gradually cultivate the practices of Bodhisattvas so they will quickly realize unsurpassed, proper and equal Bodhi.'

"The tenth great vow: 'I vow that in a future life when I attain Bodhi, I shall cause sentient beings who fall into the hands of the law and are bound, interrogated, whipped, fettered, imprisoned, sentenced to execution, or subjected to endless disasters, hardships, abuse, and humiliation so that they are torn by grief and distress and

4

suffering in body and mind, to obtain, upon hearing my name, liberation from all worry and suffering by means of my blessings, virtue, and awesome spiritual power.'

"The eleventh great vow: 'I vow that in a future life when I attain Bodhi, I shall cause all sentient beings who are so plagued by hunger and thirst that they create all kinds of bad karma in their quest for food, upon hearing my name and single-mindedly accepting and maintaining it, to be filled with delicious food and drink and afterward, by means of the flavor of Dharma, to settle in ultimate peace and happiness.'

"The twelfth great vow: 'I vow that in a future life when I attain Bodhi, if there are sentient beings who are poor and without clothes so that day and night they are troubled by mosquitoes and flies, and by cold and heat, upon hearing my name and single-mindedly accepting and maintaining it, they shall obtain all kinds of fine and wonderful garments that accord with their tastes, as well as a variety of precious adornments, flower garlands, fragrant balms, and the enjoyments of music and various kinds of talents, so that all their hearts' delights will be fulfilled.'

"Mañjuśrī, these are the twelve sublime and wonderful vows that the World Honored One, Medicine Master Vaiḍūrya Light Tathāgata, One of Proper and Equal Enlightenment, made while cultivating the Bodhisattva Way.

"Moreover, Mañjuśrī, if I were to speak for an eon or more about the great vows made by the World Honored One, Medicine Master Vaiḍūrya Light Tathāgata, when he practiced the Bodhisattva Way and about the merit, virtue, and adornments of his Buddhaland, I could not finish.

"That Buddhaland has always been completely pure; there are no women, no evil destinies, and no sounds of suffering. The ground is made of *vaiḍūrya*, with golden cords lining the roads. The city walls, towers, palace pavilions, studios, windows, and latticework are all made of the seven treasures. The merit, virtue, and adornments of this land are identical to those of the Western Land of Ultimate Bliss.

"Residing in that land are two Bodhisattvas Mahā-sattvas; the first is called Universally Radiant Sunlight, and the second, Universally Radiant Moonlight. They are the leaders among the immeasurable, uncountable hosts of Bodhisattvas in that land and will be the successors to that Buddha. They are able to maintain the precious treasury of the Proper Dharma of the World Honored One, Medicine Master Vaiḍūrya Light Tathāgata. Therefore, Mañjuśrī, all good men and women who have faith should vow to be born in that Buddha's land."

At that time, the World Honored One again spoke to the Pure Youth Mañjuśrī saying, "Mañjuśrī, there are living beings who don't distinguish good from evil, who indulge in greed and stinginess, and who know nothing of giving or its rewards. They are stupid, ignorant, and lack the foundation of faith. They accumulate much wealth and many treasures and ardently guard them. When they see a beggar coming, they feel displeased. When they have to practice an act of charity that does not benefit themselves, they feel as though they were cutting a piece of flesh from their body, and they suffer deep and painful regret.

"There are other innumerable avaricious and miserly

living beings who hoard money and necessities that they don't use even for themselves, how much less for their parents, wives, or servants, or for beggars! At the end of their lives, such beings will be reborn among the hungry ghosts or animals. If they heard the name of that Buddha, Medicine Master Vaiḍūrya Light Tathāgata, in their former human existence, and they recall that Tathāgata's name for the briefest moment while they are in the evil destinies, they will immediately be reborn in the human realm. Moreover, they will remember their past lives and will dread the sufferings of the evil destinies. They will not delight in worldly pleasures, but will rejoice in giving and praise others who give. They will not begrudge giving whatever they have. Gradually, to those who come to beg, they will be able to give away their own head, eyes, hands, feet, and even their entire body, to say nothing of their money and property!

"Moreover, Mañjuśrī, there are beings who, although they study under the Tathāgata, nonetheless violate the *śīla*. Others, although they do not violate the *śīla*, nonetheless transgress the rules and regulations. Others, although they do not violate the *śīla* or rules and regulations, nonetheless destroy their own proper views. Others, although they do not destroy their own proper views, nonetheless neglect learning, so they are unable to understand the profound meaning of the Sutras that the Buddha speaks. Others, although they are learned, nonetheless give rise to overweening pride. Shadowed by overweening pride, they justify themselves and disparage others, slander the Proper Dharma, and join the retinue of demons.

"Such fools act on their misguided views and further, cause immeasurable millions of beings to fall into pits of great danger. These beings will drift endlessly in the realms of the hells, the animals, and the ghosts. But if they hear the name of Medicine Master Vaiḍūrya Light Tathāgata, they will be able to renounce their evil practices and cultivate wholesome Dharmas, and thereby avoid falling into the evil destinies. If those who have fallen into the evil destinies because they could not renounce their evil practices and cultivate wholesome Dharmas, by the awesome power of the past vows of that Tathāgata, get to hear his name for only a moment, then after they pass out of that existence, they will be reborn again as human beings. They will hold proper views and will be ever vigorous. Their minds will be well-regulated and joyful, enabling them to renounce their families and leave the householder's life. They will take up and maintain study of the Tathāgata's Dharma without any violation. They will have proper views and erudition; they will understand profound meanings and yet be free from overweening pride. They will not slander the Proper Dharma and will never join the ranks of demons. They will progressively cultivate the practices of Bodhisattvas and will soon bring them to perfection.

"Moreover, Mañjuśrī, if there are sentient beings who harbor stinginess, greed, and jealousy, who praise themselves and disparage others, they will fall into the three evil destinies for countless thousands of years where they will undergo intense suffering. After undergoing intense suffering, at the end of their lives they will be born in the world as oxen, horses, camels, and donkeys that are constantly beaten, afflicted by thirst and hunger, and made to carry heavy burdens along the roads. Or they may be reborn among lowly people, as slaves or servants who are always ordered around by others and who never for a moment feel at ease.

"If such beings, in their former lives as humans, heard the name of the World Honored One, Medicine Master Vaiḍūrya Light Tathāgata, and by this good cause are able to remember it and sincerely take refuge with that Buddha, then, by means of the Buddha's spiritual power, they will be liberated from all sufferings. They will be endowed with keen faculties, and they will be wise and erudite. They will always seek the supreme Dharmas and encounter good friends. They will eternally sever the nets of demons and smash the shell of ignorance. They will dry up the river of afflictions and be liberated from birth, old age, sickness, death, anxiety, grief, suffering, and vexation.

"Moreover, Mañjuśrī, there may be beings who de-light in perversity and engage in legal disputes, bringing trouble to others as well as themselves. In their actions, speech, and thoughts, they create ever-increasing amounts of evil karma. Never willing to benefit and forgive others, they scheme to harm one another instead. They pray to the spirits of the mountain forests, trees, and graves. They kill living beings in order to make sacrifices of blood and flesh to the *yakṣa* and *rākṣasa* ghosts. They write down the names of their enemies and make images of them, and then they hex those names and images with evil mantras. They summon paralysis ghosts, cast hexes, or command corpse-raising ghosts to kill or injure their enemies.

"However, if the victims hear the name of Medicine Master Vaiḍūrya Light Tathāgata, then all those evil things will lose their power to do harm. The evildoers will become kind to one another. They will attain benefit, peace, and happiness and no longer cherish thoughts of malice, affliction, or enmity. Everyone will rejoice and feel content with what they have. Instead of encroaching upon each other, they will seek to benefit one another.

"Moreover, Mañjuśrī, there may be those among the fourfold assembly of Bhikshus, Bhikshunis, Upasakas and Upasikas, as well as other good men and women of pure faith, who accept and uphold the eight precepts either for one year or for three months, practicing and studying them. With these good roots, they may vow to be born in the Western Land of Ultimate Bliss where the Buddha of Limitless Life dwells, to hear the Proper Dharma, but their resolve may not be firm. However, if they hear the name of the World Honored One, Medicine Master Vaiḍūrya Light Tathāgata, then as the end of their lives draws near, before them will appear eight great Bodhisattvas, whose names are: Mañjuśrī Bodhisattva, The Bodhisattva Who Observes the Sounds of the World, Great Strength Bodhisattva, Inexhaustible Intention Bodhisattva, Jewelled Udumbara Flower Bodhisattva, Medicine King Bodhisattva, Medicine Superior Bodhisattva, and Maitreya Bodhisattva. Those eight great Bodhisattvas will appear in space to show them the way, and they will naturally be born by transformation in that land, amid precious flowers of a myriad colors.

"Or they may be born in the heavens due to this cause. Although reborn in the heavens, their original good roots will not be exhausted and so they will not fall into the evil destinies again. When their life in the heavens ends, they will be born among people again. They may be wheel-turning kings, reigning over the four continents with awesome virtue and ease, bringing uncountable hundreds of thousands of living beings to abide in the practice of the ten good deeds. Or they may be born as *kṣatriyas*, Brahmans, laymen, or sons of honorable families. They will be wealthy, with storehouses filled to overflowing. Handsome in appearance, they will be surrounded by a great retinue of relatives. They will be intelligent and wise, courageous and valiant, like great and awesome knights. If a woman hears the name of the World Honored One, Medicine Master Vaiḍūrya Light Tathāgata, and sincerely cherishes it, in the future she will never again be born as a female.

"Moreover, Mañjuśrī, when Medicine Master Vaiḍūrya Light Tathāgata attained Bodhi, by the power of his past vows he contemplated all the sentient beings who were undergoing various kinds of sicknesses and sufferings. Some suffered from diseases such as emaciation, atrophy, severe thirst, or yellow fever; others were harmed by paralysis ghosts or by poisonous hexes; some died naturally when young, while others experienced untimely deaths. He wished to dispel all their sicknesses and sufferings, and to fulfill their wishes."

At that time, the World Honored One entered a samādhi called "extinguishing the suffering and distress of all beings." After he entered this samādhi, a great light came forth from his flesh-cowl. From amid that light he proclaimed this magnificent *dhāraṇī*:

Na mo bo qie fa di. Bi sha she. Ju lu bi liu li. Bo la po. He la she ye. Da tuo jie duo ye. E la he di. San miao san pu tuo ye. Da zhi tuo nan. Bi sha shi. Bi sha shi. Bi sha she. San mo jie di. Suo he.

After he had spoken that mantra from amid the light, the earth trembled and emitted great light. All beings' sicknesses and sufferings were cast off, and they felt peaceful and happy.

"Mañjuśrī, if you see a man (or a woman) who is ill, you should single-mindedly and frequently clean and bathe him and rinse his mouth. Provide him with food, medicine, or water that is free of insects, over any of which the *dhāraṇī* has been recited 108 times. After the sick person has taken it, all his sicknesses and sufferings will be gone. If this person has a wish, he should recite this mantra with utmost sincerity. Then he will obtain whatever he wished for, and his life will be prolonged and free from illness. At the end of his life, he will be reborn in that Buddha's land. He will become irreversible and will ultimately attain Bodhi. Therefore, Mañjuśrī, if there are men and women who, with utmost sincerity, diligently worship and make offerings to Medicine Master Vaiḍūrya Light Tathāgata, they should always recite this mantra and never forget it.

"Moreover, Mañjuśrī, men or women of pure faith, who have heard all the names of Medicine Master Vaiḍūrya Light Tathāgata, One of Proper and Equal Enlightenment, should recite and uphold them. In the early morning, after brushing their teeth and bathing, they should make offerings of fragrant flowers, incense, perfumed balms, and various kinds of music before an image of that Buddha. They should personally write out this

Sutra or ask others to do so, and they should single-mindedly and constantly recite it. If they listen to explanations of its meaning from a Dharma Master, they should make offerings to him of all necessities, so that he is without the slightest want. In this way, they will receive the mindful protection of the Buddhas. All of their wishes will be fulfilled, and they will ultimately attain Bodhi."

At that time, the Pure Youth Mañjuśrī said to the Buddha, "World Honored One, I vow that in the Dharma-Image Age, using various expedient means, I shall enable good men and women of pure faith to hear the name of the World Honored One, Medicine Master Vaiḍūrya Light Tathāgata. Even during their sleep, I will awaken them with this Buddha's name.

"World Honored One, there may be those who accept and uphold this Sutra, read and recite it, explain its meanings for others, write it out themselves, or tell others to write it out. They may revere it by making offerings of various flowers, paste incense, powdered incense, stick incense, flower garlands, necklaces, banners, canopies, and music. They may make bags of five-colored thread in which to keep the Sutra. They may sweep clean a place and arrange a high altar on which to place this Sutra. At that time, the Four Heavenly Kings with their retinues and other innumerable hundreds of thousands of gods will come to that place to worship and protect it.

"World Honored One, it should be known that if, in the places where this precious Sutra circulates, people can accept and uphold it, then due to the merit and virtue of the past vows of that World Honored One, Medicine Master Vaiḍūrya Light Tathāgata, because they have

13

heard his name, none of those people will meet with untimely death. In addition, none of them will be robbed of his vital energy by evil ghosts and spirits. Those people whose vital energies have already been robbed will have their health restored, and they will be happy and at peace in body and mind."

The Buddha told Mañjuśrī, "So it is, so it is! It is exactly as you say. Mañjuśrī, if there are good men and women of pure faith who wish to make offerings to that World Honored One, Medicine Master Vaiḍūrya Light Tathāgata, they should first make an image of that Buddha and arrange a pure and clean dais on which to place the image. Then they should strew all kinds of flowers, burn various incenses, and adorn the place with a variety of banners and streamers. For seven days and seven nights they should hold the eight precepts and eat pure food. Having bathed until clean and fragrant, they should put on clean clothes. Their minds should be undefiled, without thoughts of anger and malice. Toward all sentient beings, they should cherish thoughts of benevolence, peace, kindness, compassion, joy, giving, and equanimity.

"Playing musical instruments and singing praises, they should circumambulate to the right of the Buddha's image. Moreover, they should recall the merit and virtue of that Tathāgata's past vows. They should read and recite this Sutra, ponder its meaning, and lecture on and explain it. Then they will obtain whatever they seek: Those who seek long life will attain longevity; those who seek wealth will gain wealth; those who seek an official position will obtain it; and those who seek a son or a daughter will have one.

"Moreover, if a person who suddenly has nightmares, sees ill omens, notices strange birds flocking together, or perceives many uncanny events in his dwelling can worship and make offerings of many fine things to that World Honored One, Medicine Master Vaiḍūrya Light Tathāgata, then the nightmares, ill omens, and inauspicious things will disappear and will no longer trouble him.

"When a person is endangered by water, fire, knives, or poison; or finds himself on a steep cliff or in a dangerous place; or faces fierce elephants, lions, tigers, wolves, bears, poisonous snakes, scorpions, centipedes, millipedes, mosquitoes, gnats, or other frightful things, if he can single-mindedly recollect, worship, and make offerings to that Buddha, he will be liberated from all those frightful things. When other countries invade or when there are thieves or riots, if a person can recollect and worship that Tathāgata, then he will be free of all of these as well.

"Moreover, Mañjuśrī, there may be good men and women of pure faith who, all their lives, do not worship other gods, but single-mindedly take refuge with the Buddha, the Dharma, and the Saṅgha. They accept and uphold precepts, such as the five precepts, the ten precepts, the four hundred precepts of a Bodhisattva, the two hundred and fifty precepts of a Bhikshu, or the five hundred precepts of a Bhikshuni. Perhaps they have violated some of the precepts they received and are afraid of falling into the evil destinies. If they concentrate on reciting that Buddha's name and worship and make offerings to him, they definitely will not be reborn in the three evil destinies.

"If there is a woman about to give birth who suffers great pain, if she sincerely recites his name and worships, praises, venerates, and makes offerings to that Tathāgata, all her sufferings will be dispelled. The newborn child will be sound and healthy, and will have upright features. Seeing him will make people happy. He will be keen and intelligent, peaceful and secure, and with few ailments, and no evil spirit will come to rob him of his vitality."

At that time the World Honored One said to Ananda, "The merit and virtue of the World Honored One, Medicine Master Vaiḍūrya Light Tathāgata, which I have just extolled, is the extremely profound practice of all Buddhas. It is difficult to fathom and to comprehend. Do you believe it or not?"

Ananda said, "Greatly virtuous World Honored One, I have absolutely no doubts regarding the Sutras spoken by the Tathāgata. Why? Because all Buddhas' karmas of body, speech, and mind are pure. World Honored One, the sun and moon could fall, Wonderfully High, the king of mountains, could be toppled or shaken, but the words of the Buddhas never change.

"World Honored One, there are sentient beings deficient in faith who hear about the extremely profound practices of all Buddhas and think to themselves, 'How could one obtain such supreme merit and benefit merely by reciting the name of a single Buddha, Medicine Master Vaiḍūrya Light Tathāgata?' Due to this lack of faith, they give rise to slander. During the long night, they lose great benefit and joy and fall into the evil destinies, where they wander ceaselessly."

The Buddha told Ananda, "If these sentient beings hear the name of the World Honored One, Medicine

Master Vaiḍūrya Light Tathāgata, and sincerely accept and uphold it without any doubts, they cannot possibly fall into the evil destinies.

"Ananda, this is the extremely profound practice of all Buddhas which is difficult to believe and to understand! You should know that your ability to accept this comes from the awesome power of the Tathāgata. Ananda, all Hearers, Solitarily Enlightened Ones, and the Bodhisattvas who have not yet ascended to the Grounds are incapable of believing and understanding this Dharma as it really is. Only the Bodhisattvas who are destined in one life to attain Buddhahood are capable of understanding.

"Ananda, it is difficult to obtain a human body. It is also difficult to have faith in and to revere the Triple Jewel. It is even more difficult to be able to hear the name of the World Honored One, Medicine Master Vaiḍūrya Light Tathāgata. Ananda, Medicine Master Vaiḍūrya Light Tathāgata possesses boundless Bodhisattva practices, limitless skillful expedients, and immeasurably vast, great vows. If I were to speak extensively of those for an eon or more, the eon would soon end, but that Buddha's practices, vows, and skillful expedients have no end!"

At that time within the assembly, a Bodhisattva Mahāsattva named One Who Rescues and Liberates arose from his seat, bared his right shoulder, knelt with his right knee on the ground, leaned forward with his palms joined together, and said to the Buddha, "Greatly virtuous World Honored One! During the Dharma Image Age, there will be living beings afflicted with various diseases, emaciated from chronic illnesses, unable to eat or drink, their throats parched and their lips dry. Such a being sees darkness gathering all around him as the signs of death appear. While lying in bed, surrounded by his weeping parents, relatives, and friends, he sees the messengers of Yama leading his spirit before that king of justice. Every sentient being has spirits that stay with him throughout his life. They record his every deed, both good and evil, to present to Yama, the king of justice. At that time, King Yama interrogates this person in order to tally his karma and mete out judgement according to his good and evil deeds.

"At that time, if the sick person's relatives and friends, on his behalf, can take refuge with the World Honored One, Medicine Master Vaiḍūrya Light Tathāgata, and request members of the Saṅgha to recite this Sutra, to light seven layers of lamps, and to hang up the five-colored banners for prolonging life, then it is possible for his spirit to return. As if in a dream, the person will see everything very clearly himself.

"If his spirit returns after seven, twenty-one, thirty-five, or forty-nine days, he will feel as if awakened from a dream and will remember the retributions that he underwent for his good and bad karma. Having personally witnessed the retributions of his own karma, he will never again do any evil, even if his very life is endangered. Therefore, good men and women of pure faith should accept and uphold the name of Medicine Master Vaiḍūrya Light Tathāgata and, according to their capability, worship and make offerings to him."

At that time, Ananda asked the Bodhisattva Who Rescues and Liberates, "Good man, how should we worship and make offerings to the World Honored One, Medicine Master Vaiḍūrya Light Tathāgata? And how should we make the banners and lamps that prolong life?"

The Bodhisattva Who Rescues and Liberates said, "Greatly Virtuous One, if there is a sick person who wishes to be freed from sickness and suffering, for his sake one should accept and uphold the eight precepts for seven days and seven nights, and make offerings to the Bhikshu Sangha of as many items of food, drink, and other necessities as are in his power to give.

"During the six periods of the day and night one should worship, practice the Way, and make offerings to the World Honored One, Medicine Master Vaiḍūrya Light Tathāgata. Read and recite this Sutra forty-nine times, light forty-nine lamps, and make seven images of that Tathāgata. In front of each image place seven lamps, each as large as a cartwheel. These lamps must be kept burning continuously for forty-nine days. Hang up five-colored banners that are forty-nine spans long. Liberate a variety of living creatures, as many as forty-nine species. Then the sick one will be able to surmount the danger and will not suffer an untimely death or be held by evil ghosts.

"Furthermore, Ananda, in the case of *kṣatriya* princes who are due to be anointed on the crowns of their heads, at a time when calamity arises, such as pestilence among the population, invasion by foreign countries, rebellion within their territories, unusual changes in the stars, a solar or lunar eclipse, unseasonal winds and rains, or prolonged drought, those *kṣatriya* princes should bring forth an attitude of kindness and compassion toward all sentient beings and grant amnesty to all prisoners. They should follow the above-mentioned methods to make offerings to that World Honored One, Medicine Master Vaiḍūrya Light Tathāgata. Due to these good roots and

19

the power of that Tathāgata's past vows, the country will be safe and peaceful, the winds and rains will be timely, the crops will ripen, and all sentient beings will be blissful and free of disease. Within this country there will be no violence, nor any *yakṣas* or other spirits that harm sentient beings, and all evil omens will vanish.

"The *kṣatriya* princes who are due to be anointed on the crowns of their heads will enjoy longer lives and good health, and they will be at ease and free from illness. Ananda, if the queens, the princes, the ministers or court counselors, the ladies of the palace, the provincial officials or the common people suffer from diseases or other difficulties, they should also hang up five-colored spiritual banners, light lamps and keep them burning, liberate living creatures, strew flowers of various colors, and burn precious incense. Then those people will be cured of their diseases and relieved of their difficulties."

Then Ananda asked the Bodhisattva Who Rescues and Liberates, "Good man, how can a life that has come to an end be prolonged?"

The Bodhisattva Who Rescues and Liberates answered, "Greatly Virtuous One, did you not hear the Tathāgata say that there are nine kinds of untimely death? That is why people are exhorted to make life-prolonging banners and lamps and to cultivate all kinds of blessings. Through such cultivation of blessings, they will be freed from suffering and adversity for the rest of their lives."

Ananda asked, "What are the nine kinds of untimely death?"

The Bodhisattva Who Rescues and Liberates said, "There may be living beings who, although not seriously ill, have neither medicine nor a doctor to treat them, or else they meet a doctor who gives them the wrong medicine; consequently, they meet with an untimely death. Some of them believe in worldly cults, whose deviant teachers frighten them with false prophecies. Unable to set their minds at ease, they consult oracles to find out what calamities are in store for them. In order to propitiate the spirits, they kill various creatures. They pray to *wang liang* ghosts for aid and protection. Although they wish to prolong their lives, their efforts are to no avail. They deludedly hold to wrong beliefs and perverse views. Thus they meet with an untimely death and fall into the hells, never to come out. This is the first kind of untimely death.

"The second kind of untimely death is to be executed at the hands of the law. The third kind is to hunt for sport, to indulge in drinking and lust, or to become excessively dissipated, and then to be waylaid by nonhuman beings that rob one's essence and energy. The fourth is to be burned to death; the fifth is to drown; the sixth is to be devoured by wild beasts; the seventh is to fall from a steep cliff; the eighth is to be harmed by poison, voodoo, evil mantras, or corpse-raising ghosts; the ninth is to die from hunger and thirst. These are the nine kinds of untimely deaths generally spoken of by the Tathāgata. There are also innumerable other kinds which cannot all be spoken of here.

"Moreover, Ananda, King Yama keeps track of the karmic records of all the inhabitants of the world. If there are beings who are not filial to their parents, who commit the Five Rebellious Acts, who revile the Triple Jewel, who destroy the laws of the country, or who violate the precept of truthfulness, then Yama, the king of justice,

21

examines and punishes them according to the severity of their offenses. Therefore, I encourage people to light lamps and make banners, to liberate beings and cultivate blessings so that they can overcome suffering and peril and forestall all disasters."

At that time, twelve great *yakṣa* generals were present in the assembly. They were: General Kumbhīra, General Vajra, General Mihira, General Aṇḍīra, General Anila, General Saṇḍira, General Indra, General Pajra, General Makura, General Kinnara, General Catura, and General Vikarāla.

These twelve great *yakṣa* generals, each with a retinue of seven thousand *yakṣas*, simultaneously raised their voices and addressed the Buddha, "World Honored One! Today, by relying on the Buddha's awesome power, we are able to hear the name of the World Honored One, Medicine Master Vaiḍūrya Light Tathāgata! As a result, we are no longer afraid of the evil destinies. All of us are of one mind to take refuge with the Buddha, the Dharma, and the Saṅgha to the end of our lives. We vow to support all living beings and to benefit them, so that they may live in peace and happiness. In whatever cities, villages, countries, or secluded forests this Sutra circulates, or wherever people accept and uphold the name of Medicine Master Vaiḍūrya Light Tathāgata and venerate and make offerings to him, we, together with our retinues, will guard and protect them, deliver them from all distress, and fulfill all their wishes. If a person wishes to dispel illnesses and difficulties, he should read or recite this Sutra and tie a five-colored thread into knots, forming the letters of our names. He should untie the knots when his wishes have been fulfilled."

At that time, the World Honored One praised the great *yakṣa* generals, saying, "Good indeed, good indeed, mighty *yakṣa* generals! All of you who want to repay the kindness of the World Honored One, Medicine Master Vaiḍūrya Light Tathāgata, should always benefit beings and bring peace and happiness to them in this way."

Then Ananda said to the Buddha, "World Honored One, what should we call this teaching? How should we uphold it?"

The Buddha told Ananda, "This teaching is called, 'The Merit and Virtue of the Past Vows of Medicine Master Vaiḍūrya Light Tathāgata.' It is also called 'Twelve Spiritual Generals' Vows to Use Spiritual Mantras to Benefit Living Beings.' It is also called, 'Eradicating All Karmic Obstacles.' You should uphold it in this way."

When the Bhagavan had finished speaking, all the Bodhisattvas Mahāsattvas, great Hearers, kings, ministers, Brahmans, laypeople, gods, dragons, *yakṣas, gandharvas, asuras, garuḍas, kinnaras, mahoragas,* humans, and non-human beings, and all the great assembly, on hearing what the Buddha had said, were greatly delighted. They received it with faith and respectfully practiced it.

End of the *Sutra of the Merit and Virtue of the Past Vows of Medicine Master Vaiḍūrya Light Tathāgata.*

Medicine Master Buddha

Sutra of the Merit and Virtue of the Past Vows of Medicine Master Vaiḍūrya Light Tathāgata

Explained by the Venerable Master Hua
in 1983 at Gold Wheel Monastery in Los Angeles

ŚĀKYAMUNI BUDDHA CAME TO the Sahā world in order to help living beings resolve the problem of birth and death. He was born into a royal family, but he renounced the wealth of the kingdom and left his home in order to pursue the Truth. After he attained Buddhahood beneath the Bodhi Tree, he contemplated the living beings in the Sahā world and discovered that we have the deepest affinities with two Buddhas—Medicine Master Vaiḍūrya Light Tathāgata in the East and Amitābha Tathāgata in the West.

Medicine Master Vaiḍūrya Light Tathāgata is the Buddha of the Land of Vaiḍūrya Light in the East. This Buddha bestows blessings and long life on people and helps them in times of disaster and difficulty. Amitābha Buddha of the Land of Ultimate Bliss in the West made a vow that whoever recites his name single-mindedly will be able to take his or her karma along and be reborn from a lotus in his Buddhaland, and that when his or her lotus opens he or she will see the Buddha and awaken to the patience of nonproduction.

The "Mantra of the Two Buddhas" says,

Two Buddhas proclaim and transform
  in the Sahā world—
Akṣobhya in the East, Amitābha in the West.

Although Akṣobhya (Medicine Master) Buddha is in the Vaiḍūrya Land and Amitābha Buddha is in the Land of Ultimate Bliss, both of these Buddhas teach and transform the living beings of the Sahā world. They have deep affinities with each and every one of us. Medicine Master Tathāgata is also known as "Medicine Master Buddha Who Quells Disasters and Lengthens Life;" Amitābha Tathāgata is known as both the "Buddha of Limitless Life" (Amitāyus) and the "Buddha of Limitless Light" (Amitābha).

If you are mindful of Medicine Master Buddha, he will bestow blessings and long life upon you and save you from disasters, illnesses, and offenses. He fulfills the wishes of all living beings. Amitābha Buddha enables beings to be reborn in the Land of Ultimate Bliss. If you wish to be reborn in that land, simply recite Amitābha Buddha's name. If you wish to be born in the Vaiḍūrya Land, then recite the name of Medicine Master Vaiḍūrya Light Tathāgata.

During their lives, people would like to avert disasters and live to a ripe old age. At death, they hope to be reborn in the Land of Ultimate Bliss. Therefore, in Buddhism, there are red plaques for extending life, which are associated with Medicine Master Buddha Who Quells Disasters and Lengthens Life. This Buddha's light shines upon your life-source. If you wish to be reborn in the Land of Ultimate Bliss when you die, then you can recite "Namo Amitābha

Buddha." As you can see, we are basically inseparable from these two Buddhas.

Yet we don't recognize or know very much about these two Buddhas. We might want to be mindful of them, but we don't even know their names. That's why Sākyamuni Buddha introduced them to us, telling us about their names, their vows, and their merit and virtue. Hence the name of this Sutra is the *Sutra of the Merit and Virtue of the Past Vows of Medicine Master Vaiḍūrya Light Tathāgata.*

"Medicine Master Vaiḍūrya Light" is the name of this Buddha. Tathāgata is one of the ten titles of all Buddhas. "Past Vows" refers to the vows to achieve Bodhi that Medicine Master Buddha made before he became a Buddha. If we sincerely make vows, we will certainly reap the fruits of those vows—they won't be in vain. Vows are also a form of karma. If we make good vows, we will reap good results; bad vows bring bad results. Each person must make his own vows of his own initiative. Once we have made vows, there will be a driving power pushing us to accomplish those vows. Medicine Master Buddha made wholesome vows in his past lives, so he accomplished wholesome karma and reaped wholesome results.

His vows are wholesome because he made them for all living beings. He didn't vow, "When I become a Buddha, I'll enjoy my blessings and forget about other living beings." Having attained the greatest happiness, the Buddha wants to share it with all beings. He perfected his wholesome karma by practicing the Bodhisattva path in life after life. He made a great Bodhi resolve to benefit, enlighten, and rescue all beings. Forgetting themselves and thinking only of living beings, Bodhisattvas make wholesome vows,

27

create wholesome karma, and reap the wholesome result of Buddhahood. When they become Buddhas, they are not arrogant. A Buddha is just the same as living beings, except that he has wisdom. He has truly left confusion behind and returned to enlightenment.

We create karma in our every word and deed, and almost all of it is bad. We might have an occasional good thought, but it is too weak to overcome our bad thoughts. If we were to tally up all our karma on the computer, we would find more bad karma than good. That's why our lives get worse and worse. In each life, due to the impure karma we have created, we meet hard times and end up lost and alone. Unlike the Buddha, we haven't always made wholesome vows, cultivated wholesome karma, and reaped wholesome results. Since the evil in our minds outweighs the goodness, we fall lower and lower in each successive life. When we try to make wholesome vows, our selfishness gets in the way. Sometimes we do good deeds, but our real motive is just to present a good image. Thus, the karma we create is never wholly good. Since our good intentions are always polluted by selfish thoughts, we experience more suffering than happiness in our lives.

Our happiness is not real. It is not the genuine happiness that arises from the virtues of "permanence, bliss, true self, and purity" of our inherent natures. The things we find happiness in are not genuine or lasting. When we go dancing, drink wine, or go to the theater, we are "turning our backs on enlightenment and uniting with the dust," deluding ourselves into thinking that we are happy.

"Is there no happiness in the world, then?" you ask. Think it over. All forms of worldly happiness are indirect causes of suffering. Take clothing, food, and shelter, for instance. People like to dress up in style. But when you put on fancy and expensive clothes, they turn into a yoke around your neck. You can't move around freely, or stand naturally, or sit or lie down comfortably either. Why not? Because you want to protect your fancy, expensive outfit. Ha! Just think about it: A human being, the highest of all creatures, becomes a slave to his clothes!

People like to eat good food, but even the most delicious food decomposes once it is ingested. If you asked people to regurgitate their food and eat it again, no one would do it.

As for shelter, there's a saying:

One may have ten thousand mansions,
But one doesn't need more than eight feet
    of space to sleep in at night.
One may have ten thousand acres of fertile fields,
But one can only eat three meals a day.

Why should you work so frantically all day long, without a moment's rest, for the sake of clothing, food, and shelter? When death arrives, you say to the Ghost of Impermanence, "Wait, I haven't finished taking care of my affairs. Can't you let me have a little more time?" The Ghost of Impermanence shakes his head and says, "Sorry, I can't let you live even a minute longer." And so off you go to die. What's the point of it all? Failing to see things the way they really are, we spend our lives madly pursuing fame and fortune. This is where we differ from the Buddhas.

The Buddha has a clear view of everything. He has seen through everything and put it down, and so he has attained comfort and ease. When he saw through every-thing, he vowed to benefit living beings and practice the Bodhisattva Way.

Merit and virtue. Merit is created externally, while virtue is accumulated internally. One creates merit by building temples, repairing bridges or roads, or doing other work to benefit others. Virtue exists within one's self and doesn't rely on anything external. A virtuous person doesn't have a bad conscience. He has no reason to feel ashamed before the heavens or before other people. He doesn't cheat others or himself. In everything he does, he creates outer merit and amasses inner virtue. A saying about virtue goes,

> *Good done in the hope that others will notice*
> *is not genuine good.*
> *Evil done in the fear that others will find out*
> *is truly great evil.*

Don't boast about yourself, saying, "I've done good deeds. I've received the five precepts, the eight precepts, and the Bodhisattva precepts!" Virtuous deeds are done without others knowing. If you want others to notice your good deeds, you are not virtuous. If you try to cover up your bad deeds, then your offenses are great indeed.

Buddhists should not be boastful or competitive, saying, "I've done many good deeds and made lots of donations! I really do a lot to support Buddhism!" People with such an attitude are not fit to be Dharma-protectors. Therefore, in studying the teachings, we should remember this point. We should value genuine practice, not false publicity. This is very important. As Buddhists, we must be models for the world. If we have integrity and hold to our principles, other people will respect us and be influenced by us. That is merit and virtue.

"Sutra" refers to the eternal Dharma, to teachings that are not subject to change. Since the Sutras are the teachings of sages, we should never delete or add even a single word to them. The word "Sutra" has many meanings, but in general, they do not go beyond the four meanings of "stringing together," "attracting," being "constant," and being "a standard."

The Four Meanings of "Sutra":

1. "Stringing together:" The principles and meanings spoken by the Buddha are strung together from the beginning to the end.

2. "Attracting" means gathering in all living beings.

3. Being "constant" means never changing from ancient times to the present. Whether the Sutras are spoken by the Buddhas of the past, present, or future, they are the same .

4. Being "a standard:" A Sutra is a standard followed by all Buddhas and all living beings of the past, present, and future. By definition, a "standard" is honored by all throughout time.

The word Sutra has the meaning of "a chalk-line," for it is like the marking line that carpenters used in ancient times for making straight lines. Sutra also means "a bubbling spring," for it is like water gushing forth from a spring. Although the word "Sutra" contains a great many principles, you should remember the general meanings discussed above.

Now let us continue to explain the words of the title,

"Sutra of the Merit and Virtue of the Past Vows of Medicine Master Vaiḍūrya Light Tathāgata." "Master" refers to the Buddha, who is a great king of physicians, one who can heal the sicknesses of all people. No matter what sort of incurable disease you have, the Buddha can certainly cure you. Even if you are supposed to die, he can bring you back to life. Therefore, he is the "Medicine Master."

"Vaiḍūrya" is a translucent substance. It is also the name of Medicine Master Buddha's land of reward, where he is the teaching host. His body, which is made of *vaiḍūrya*, is pure and lustrous both inside and out. This Buddha thoroughly understands all the various kinds of medicines. In ancient China, the Emperor Shennong *[c. 2838 B.C.]* was said to have tasted all the various medicinal herbs. His body was also as if transparent. When he ingested a medicine, he could observe its effects in his stomach and see what channels the medicine travelled to. He tasted all the medicinal herbs and classified them as sour, sweet, bitter, pungent, or salty; as cold, hot, warm, or neutral in nature; and as poisonous or nontoxic. "Light": this Buddha's body has an inner and outer radiance and is a pure, bright storehouse of light.

"Tathāgata" is one of the ten titles of a Buddha. The ten titles are: Tathāgata (Thus Come One), One Worthy of Offerings, One of Proper and Universal Knowledge, One Whose Understanding and Practice are Complete, Well Gone One Who Understands the World, Supreme Lord, Regulating Hero, Teacher of Gods and Humans, Buddha, and World Honored One. Originally, every Buddha had 100,000 titles, but that was too many for people to remember, so they were later condensed to 10,000. That was still too many, so they were reduced to 1000. But 1000 was still too numerous, so they were decreased to 100. One hundred titles were still too many, so they were reduced to only ten titles. These ten titles do not belong exclusively to any particular Buddha; every Buddha has them. All Buddhists should know these ten general designations for the Buddhas. Some people who know nothing about Buddhism think "Tathāgata Buddha" is the name of a Buddha, but actually, every Buddha can be called Tathāgata. Tathāgata ("Thus Come One") means: "Following the Way which is Thus, he comes to realize right enlightenment."

"Past Vows" refers to vows that the Buddha made in past lives, not to vows made in the present life.

Medicine Master Vaiḍūrya Light Tathāgata of the Eastern Land is also known as "Akṣobhya Buddha." Medicine Master Buddha belongs to the Vajra Division in the East. The Vajra Division emphasizes the Dharmas of Subduing, which can overcome the heavenly demons and those of external sects. The demons and externalists become subdued as soon as they see the Vajra Dharma-protectors of the Vajra Division. If you sincerely recite the Śūraṅgama Mantra, which contains Dharmas of Subduing, you will have the constant protection of 84,000 Vajra Treasury Bodhisattvas.

Sutra:

> **Thus I have heard. At one time the Bhagavan was travelling through various lands to teach living beings. He arrived at Vaiśālī [*"City of Extensive Adornments"*] and stayed beneath a tree from which music resounded. With him were eight thousand great**

Bhikshus and thirty-six thousand Bodhisattvas Mahā-
sattvas; also kings, ministers, Brahmans, lay disciples;
gods, dragons, and the rest of the eightfold division;
beings both human and non-human. The immeasurable great multitude respectfully surrounded him, and
he spoke Dharma for them.

Commentary:

Thus I have heard. The word "thus" means, "The Dharma
which is 'thus' can be believed, studied, and practiced. You
should make vows to practice according to the Dharma
which is 'thus.'" Ananda *[who recited the Sutra after the
Buddha's Nirvana]* is saying, "The Dharma spoken in this
Sutra is what I, Ananda, personally heard the Buddha
speak with his golden mouth. It is not hearsay. I myself
heard it."

The Four Matters

There were four reasons for saying "Thus I have heard,"
which the Buddha gave when Ananda asked about the
Four Matters. When the Buddha was about to enter Nirvana,
Ananda was so overcome with grief that he could only cry!
Although Ananda was a Third Stage Arhat, he was still
emotional. He couldn't bear to think that the Buddha was
going to enter Nirvana, so he wept piteously, forgetting
about everything else.

Then another Bhikshu *[Venerable Aniruddha]* re-
minded him, "You're in charge of remembering the
Dharma spoken by the Buddha. The Buddha is about to
enter Nirvana, so you'd better think things over clearly!
There are some important matters you should ask the

Buddha about before he enters Nirvana. All you know how to do is cry! What will become of us in the future?"

Hearing the Venerable One's words, Ananda collected his wits and said, "Yes, you're right, but I've been crying so hard I can't think straight. What should we ask the Buddha?"

The Venerable One said, "First of all, when we compile the Sutras in the future, how should they begin?"

Ananda replied, "Right! That's very important!"

"Second, when the Buddha is in the world, we take the Buddha as our teacher. After the Buddha enters Nirvana, whom should we take as our teacher?"

Ananda said, "Yes, that's also an important question!"

"Third, when the Buddha is in the world, all the Bhikshus dwell with the Buddha. After the Buddha enters Nirvana, with whom should we dwell?"

"That's certainly a good question!" said Ananda.

"Fourth, when the Buddha is in the world, he can subdue the evil-natured Bhikshus. After the Buddha enters Nirvana, who should discipline them?"

"These four questions are all extremely important," said Ananda. "Now I will go and ask the Buddha."

Then he went before the Buddha, knelt, placed his palms together, and said, "World Honored One, since you are about to enter Nirvana, there are some important questions I would like to ask. I hope the Buddha will compassionately answer them."

The Buddha replied, "What are your questions? You may ask them now."

"Buddha, you have spoken the Dharma for forty-nine years and expounded the Sutras in over three hundred assemblies," said Ananda, "In the future, when we compile the Sutras, how should they begin?"

The Buddha told Ananda, "Our Sutras are different from the scriptures of other religions, which begin by speaking of either existence or non-existence. You should begin the Buddhist Sutras with the four words, 'Thus I have heard,' which means, 'I, Ananda, personally heard this Dharma, which is thus; it is not hearsay.'"

Ananda said, "Okay, I will use the four words, 'Thus I have heard.' My second question is, when the Buddha is in the world, we Bhikshus take the Buddha as our teacher. Whom should we take as our teacher after the Buddha enters Nirvana?"

The Buddha said, "After I enter Nirvana, you Bhikshus should take the precepts as your teacher. The Prātimokṣa is your great teacher. If you uphold the precepts, it will be the same as when I am in the world. You should avoid all evil and practice all good deeds."

In the beginning of the Buddha's teaching career, there were no precepts, but as the Saṅgha continued to grow, complications inevitably arose. Not everyone was well-behaved. The Buddha established the precepts one by one in response to the needs of the situation. In the final compilation of the precepts, there were 250 precepts for Bhikshus, 348 precepts for Bhikshunis, ten major and forty-eight minor precepts for Bodhisattvas, ten precepts for Shramaneras (novices), and eight precepts and five precepts for laypeople. All these various categories of precepts are aimed at helping people to behave well. People who are well-behaved will be good citizens who can help others and benefit the society. Thus, the moral precepts are the basis for world peace. Therefore, Bhikshus should take the precepts as their teacher.

"Now I'll ask the third question," continued Ananda. "When the Buddha is in the world, we dwell with the Buddha. We always live and study with the Buddha. After the Buddha enters Nirvana, with whom should the Bhikshus dwell?"

The Buddha answered, "After I enter Nirvana, all the Bhikshus should dwell in the Four Applications of Mindfulness."

The Four Applications of Mindfulness:

1. Contemplating the body as impure.
2. Contemplating feelings as suffering.
3. Contemplating thoughts as impermanent.
4. Contemplating dharmas as being without self.

The first application of mindfulness is to contemplate the body as impure. "But," you say, "I take a bath and keep my body clean every day, and I put on make-up and jewelry to make it beautiful." You may adorn your body with expensive jewelry and designer clothes, but it's just like decorating a toilet; no matter how beautiful the toilet looks, it will still stink!

The nine orifices of our bodies constantly discharge impurities. There is unclean matter from the eyes, wax from the ears, mucus in the nose, and saliva and phlegm in the mouth. Together with the anus and urethra, they make up the nine orifices that discharge impurities. If you don't bathe for several days, your body begins to stink. If you eat onions and garlic, your body will smell of onions and garlic. When you drink milk, it smells of milk. If you eat beef, veal, or pork, then you'll have those odors about you.

37

If you eat dog meat, you'll smell like dog meat. You smell of whatever you eat.

"The flavor is in my mouth," you might say, "and all I have to do is brush my teeth and the flavor will be gone." Wrong! When you eat something, its flavor not only stays in your mouth, it permeates your whole body. You don't believe it? Drink a lot of milk, and you'll notice that your sweat has a milky smell to it. Since impurities are always coming from the nine orifices, what's so good about your body? Thus, you should contemplate the body as being impure. The origin of the body is unclean. It is formed of the four elements (earth, water, fire, and air) and is not real.

Second, contemplate feelings as suffering. Feelings refers to sensations. No matter how enjoyable the sensation is, it is basically suffering! Happiness is the cause of suffering. Third, contemplate thoughts as impermanent. Thoughts arise in continuous succession, one after another; they don't last. Fourth, contemplate dharmas as being without self. All dharmas (phenomena) are free of the notion of "me and mine." These are the Four Applications of Mindfulness.

Contemplate the body as impure; feelings, thoughts, and dharmas are also impure. Contemplate feelings as suffering; the body, thoughts, and dharmas are also suffering. Thoughts are impermanent, and so are the other three. Dharmas are without self, and the other three are also without self. The Four Applications of Mindfulness apply to each of body, feelings, thoughts, and dharmas. Since the time of the Buddha's Nirvana, the Bhikshus have "dwelt" in the Four Applications of Mindfulness as the Buddha instructed.

"Here is my fourth question," said Ananda. "When the Buddha is in the world, the Buddha can subdue the evil-natured Bhikshus. After the Buddha enters Nirvana, how should we deal with them?"

The Buddha said, "When you encounter an evil-natured Bhikshu, just ignore him—don't talk to him." To ignore him is a passive way of expelling him. If no one pays attention to him or argues with him, he will soon grow bored of making trouble. If you pay attention to him or try to fight with him, he will think that he is getting somewhere. But if you ignore him, he won't be able to do anything! An "evil-natured Bhikshu" is a monk who doesn't practice. Not every left-home person wants to practice.

In the past, there were all kinds of left-home people in the great monasteries of China, including former murderers, arsonists, and robbers. Some of them reformed after they left the home-life. Others assumed the guise of monks in order to escape the authorities. There were both good and bad people in the Sangha in China, and I believe that this will be the case in other places as well.

Speaking of criminals, in China, vagrants are nicknamed "naughty monkeys" and also "Thousand-handed Guanyins," because they have so many hands. They'll steal whatever catches their fancy, and then sell it and use the money to buy alcohol or drugs. Don't be naive and think that all left-home people are good. Left-home people—and that includes myself—are not necessarily good people. However, I'm trying to be good. I don't know what bad deeds I did in the past, but now I want to become a better person.

Evil-natured Bhikshus are perverse and unreasonable.

The more you argue with them, the more they enjoy it. That's why the Buddha instructed us to ignore them.

The Three Doubts of the Assembly

When Ananda first ascended the Dharma-seat—the seat where the Buddha spoke the Dharma—to begin the compilation of Sutras, there were many auspicious portents. For instance, Ananda became endowed with the thirty-two features and eighty subsidiary characteristics of a Buddha. Seeing those portents, the members of the assembly immediately had three kinds of doubts:

1. They thought that Ananda was their teacher, Śākyamuni Buddha, who had come back to life.

2. They thought that Ananda was a Buddha from another world. "Is this a Buddha who has come from another world to speak the Dharma in the Sahā world? Otherwise, why would he look like that?"

3. They thought Ananda himself had become a Buddha.

The entire assembly was startled and at a loss, but once Ananda said, "Thus I have heard," their three doubts were dispelled. He was in effect stating, "This is the Dharma that I, Ananda, personally heard Śākyamuni Buddha speak."

Even the Arhats had three doubts when they saw Ananda leading the compilation of the Sutras. As we listen to this Sutra, we may have a thousand or even ten thousand doubts! "Is this Sutra true? Did the Buddha really say this? What proof is there?" Our human brain starts plugging away, generating millions of doubts! So, you see, studying the Buddhadharma is not that easy. Why haven't we had any attainment? Too many doubts, that's why!

A cultivator should take care not to doubt.
Once you doubt, you go astray.

You shouldn't be so skeptical. You refuse to believe the truth, but you accept a false teaching right away. That's why you are utterly deluded. Once you have a doubt, you are sure to take the wrong road.

You should study the Dharma day after day and learn from the Buddha at all times. Don't be lax. If you really want to study Buddhism, you should memorize the *Śūraṅgama Sūtra*. Everyone should master this Sutra, know it inside out. If you can recite the *Śūraṅgama Sūtra* from memory, then your study of Buddhism will have been worth it. The *Śūraṅgama Sūtra* is the Buddha's most genuine and penetrating teaching. It exposes all the short-comings and weaknesses of the heterodox sects. If you understand the *Śūraṅgama Sūtra*, you will frighten the demons from the heavens and their followers in heterodox sects so much that their hair stands on end. Therefore, if you really want to support the Triple Jewel and propagate Buddhism, then you should start by studying, reciting, and explaining the *Śūraṅgama Sūtra*.

Studying Sutras and listening to lectures requires patience. Just as plants and people grow and mature day by day, just as children study in school each day, we should set aside some time each day to study the Dharma. Studying Buddhism is worth more than any amount of money you save up in the bank! In terms of your Dharma body and wisdom life, the Dharma is far more important than money. Don't take worldly wealth so seriously. When you study the Dharma, you earn a transcendental kind of wealth, which can be used in the world and which is indispensable if you want to transcend the world. So, don't look lightly upon the wealth of Dharma and of merit and virtue.

Don't take this casually! It would be best if you could find some time in your busy schedule to come listen to the Sutra lecture and investigate Buddhism every day. "But the lecture is always about the same thing," you say, "It's boring. Why do I have to listen to it every day?" No matter how busy you are, you still have to eat, dress, and sleep every day, don't you? If only you would consider listening to the Sutra as important as dressing, eating, and sleeping!

The Six Requirements

There are Six Requirements found at the beginning of each Sutra. The first is the Requirement of Faith, indicated by the word "Thus." We should have faith in Dharma which is thus, cultivate it, and attain Buddhahood by means of it.

Only by means of faith can you attain realization and derive benefit. It's like eating. If you don't believe that food can satisfy your hunger, you won't eat it and get full. Similarly, although the Dharma can lead you to Buddhahood, if you don't believe in it and cultivate it, then it's of no use. Talking about cultivation is not enough. "The Dharma is spoken; the Way is walked." You can benefit from the Dharma only if you believe in and practice it.

The second requirement, the Requirement of Hearing, is indicated by the words "I have heard." Ananda refers to himself as "I," but this "I" is selfless and unattached, perfectly fused and unimpeded. It is the true self of the inherent nature, which has seen through all things and put them down. This "I" is spoken not to others, but rather, to oneself. This "I" is wise and not deluded, and is endowed with Dharma-selecting vision, so it can deeply enter the treasury of Sutras and have wisdom like the sea. How can one obtain Dharma-selecting vision? It develops through possessing the requirements of faith and hearing. "I have faith, and I would like to listen to the Sutra," you say.

That's fine, but there must be a time—a time for listening to the lecture on the *Medicine Master Sutra*. This also refers to the time when Ananda compiled the Sutras. The words "**At one time**" fulfill the Requirement of Time. You may have faith and may wish to hear the Sutra, but if the lecture is scheduled at an inconvenient time, you still won't get to hear the Sutra.

The Bhagavan is another name for the Buddha. If you don't know what "Bhagavan" means, just remember that it's another Sanskrit name for the Buddha. In the text, the word "Bhagavan" fulfills the Requirement of a Host. The requirements of faith, hearing, and time may be satisfied, but if no one lectures on the Sutra, then what are you going to listen to? There's nothing to listen to and nothing to believe, and the time is irrelevant as well! And so a "host," a person who explains the Sutra and speaks the Dharma, is necessary.

The word "Bhagavan," when translated, has six meanings:

1. Comfortable
2. Renowned
3. Adorned
4. Resplendent
5. Auspicious
6. Honored

"Auspicious:" Chinese people like auspiciousness, especially the Cantonese. At New Year's, they always say,
"Good luck! May your wishes come true!" Although they
like to have good luck, they spend their time playing
mahjong and dancing. If you want things to be lucky and
according to your wishes, you have to recite the Buddha's
name. You also have to be good and follow the rules. If you
play mahjong, you might even lose the shirt off your back!
Now, would you call that lucky?

"Honored": The Buddha is the most honored one. If we
wish to be honored, we should learn from the Buddha, the
most venerable and perfect being, who is free of bad habits,
faults, delusions, and scattered thoughts. The Buddha's
state is much higher than that of an Arhat. The *Dharma
Flower Sutra* begins, "Thus have I heard. At one time the
Buddha dwelt on Mount Gṛdhrakūṭa, near the city of
Rājagṛha *["House of Kings"]*, together with a gathering of
great Bhikshus, twelve thousand in all. All were Arhats..."
Why were they Arhats? They "had exhausted all outflows."
One who attains the state of an Arhat no longer has any
faults, bad habits, or idle thoughts. He has put an end to
birth and death. They "had done what they had to do."
They had done everything they were supposed to do.
When the One is attained, all things are finished. They had
attained the One, so they didn't seek outside anymore.
Since they didn't seek outside, they had no more outflows.
If you like to talk, that's an outflow, as is liking to look at
things or to listen to sounds.

"But I can't keep my eyes from seeing and my ears from
hearing," you say.

That's why you haven't become a Buddha yet. You're

always running outside and forgetting to return. You aren't able to turn the light around and shine it within. Exhausting all outflows means having no faults whatsoever—you aren't greedy, you don't contend, you don't seek anything, you aren't selfish, and you don't pursue personal advantages. Affection and love are also faults, and thoughts of desire are the worst faults of all. To have exhausted all outflows means to have no thoughts of desire, thoughts of lust, or wild and deluded thoughts.

"And had no further afflictions": The Arhats no longer had any afflictions. "Having attained self-benefit": They had truly regained their inherent wisdom and gained the advantages of the Buddha's teaching. As I have said to you, "Who is the Buddha? The Buddha is a person of great wisdom. Whoever has true wisdom and is not deluded can become a Buddha." If you are still deluded and insatiably greedy, always seeking for more, fighting with everyone, being selfish and pursuing personal gain, then you haven't gained any benefit from the Dharma. Those who have attained genuine benefit do not crave external things. Gold, silver, and riches mean nothing to them. They do not know what forms, sounds, smells, tastes, and objects of touch are. Nothing can distract them. That is what is meant by "having attained self-benefit."

"They had exhausted the bonds of all existence." They had eradicated all residual habits and had escaped from all the entanglements that used to bind them. They were truly free. "And their hearts had attained self-mastery." Their hearts were carefree and at ease. However, the Buddha's state is much more advanced. That's why the Buddha is considered the most honored and venerable.

45

If we want to be like the Buddha, first we should learn not to contend, not to be greedy, not to seek, not to be selfish, and not to pursue personal advantage. But that doesn't mean saying you won't do these things, while at the same time planning to commit a robbery. Then you're only cheating yourself and others! Genuine noncontention means letting things follow their natural course. If you are not greedy, you will also let things happen naturally. As for seeking nothing, it is said, "When one reaches the state of seeking nothing, one has no worries." Worries come from seeking things. You should also be unselfish. All the troubles in the world come from selfishness and desire. Being unselfish means seeking nothing and having no emotional attachments. Not pursuing personal advantage means not thinking about your own benefit, pleasure, or comfort. Cast out all these faults, and then you can become a Buddha!

The six meanings of "Bhagavan" are very important, and Buddhists should remember them. If you don't, you won't even recognize the Buddha. It's like knowing a person. If you can recognize someone by his appearance or the sound of his voice, you can say you know him. Knowing the Buddha is the same way. If you don't even know what the Buddha's title "Bhagavan" means, you are certainly a muddled Buddhist! So, you should memorize them and be prepared to say what they are next time. I have spent so much time and energy explaining the Sutra to you; it'd be a shame if you forgot everything once the lecture was over. If you aren't able to answer my questions, then I'll know that you've been sleeping!

The Buddha **was travelling through various lands to**

teach living beings. He arrived at Vaiśālī [*"City of Extensive Adornments"*] and stayed beneath a tree from which music resounded. The Buddha teaches and transforms living beings not only in one country, but in all the countries where he has affinities.

As the Buddha was travelling around to teach living beings, he came to the large city of Vaiśālī, where he seated himself in full-lotus posture at the base of a tree which put forth music, and spoke Dharma for the multitudes. "At Vaiśālī" and "beneath a tree from which music resounded" fulfill the Requirement of a Place. Above, we had the requirements of faith, hearing, time, and host. With the requirement of a host, there is a person to speak the Sutra, but if there is no place, how can he speak? For example, if we didn't have a lecture hall, how could we hold a lecture on the *Medicine Master Sutra*? And so it is necessary to have a place. The tree from which music resounded is the location where the *Medicine Master Sutra* was spoken.

The Bhikshus and Bodhisattvas mentioned in the next passage of text fulfill the Requirement of an Audience. Once there is a lecturer and a place for the lecture, people have to go and listen. If no one went to listen to the Buddha when he spoke, his speaking would have been rather pointless. The Dharma is spoken for living beings. Each Dharma assembly has living beings who have affinities with it. For instance, you have come to this Sutra lecture because you have affinities with it. Those without affinities cannot come even if they want to. You have the chance to come listen every day now because you planted good roots during many past lives and many eons. It's not as simple as you think!

47

Since you don't realize how difficult it is to take part in a Dharma assembly, sometimes you become lazy, thinking, "The Master isn't here yet, so I think I'll just steal away for some fun." And so you go to watch a play or see a movie, or you go to a dance or a party. You waste your energy doing these things which are of no benefit. When you come to the Sutra lecture, you hear the sound of the Dharma and it lightens your worldly defilements and deluded thoughts. You study the *prajñā*-wisdom found in the Sutras. Every time you listen, you understand a little bit more.

"I already understand a lot!" you say. What's wrong with understanding a little bit more? Why do you think it's too much? I never hear you complain about having too much money! No matter how rich you are, you never think you have too much. "The more the better!" is your attitude. So why, when you study wisdom, when you study the true Dharma, are you afraid of learning too much? Isn't this delusion? Since you've never really thought about it, you simply forget what's fundamental so as to pursue the superficial; you look for what is faraway and fail to notice what's right beside you. Instead of seriously investigating the Buddhadharma, you just waste your time!

With him were eight thousand great Bhikshus. Bhikshus are men who have left the home-life. They were called "great Bhikshus" because they were virtuous and wise elders who had left home for at least twenty or thirty years. "Bhikshu" is Sanskrit and has three meanings:

1. Mendicant
2. Frightener of demons
3. Destroyer of evil

Although a mendicant is one who collects alms from others, he is not a common beggar. Common beggars sometimes obtain their food in unscrupulous ways, and they lack the spirit of equanimity. If they don't get enough food, they become afflicted. A mendicant, on the other hand, doesn't notice whether the food tastes good or not. Nor does he care whether you give him a lot or a little. He simply wants to give people the opportunity to "plant" blessings. The donor's blessings will be as bountiful as the seeds he or she sows.

A mendicant monk is free of affliction and ignorance. He carries himself with dignity and obtains food in the proper manner. When Bhikshus walk on the road, they do not stare around at random. Instead, their eyes contemplate their noses, their noses contemplate their mouths, and their mouths contemplate their hearts. They do not look at, listen to, speak about, or do anything that does not accord with propriety. Bhikshus seek alms in silence, unlike common beggars, who may stand at people's doors and say flattering things, such as, "Sir! Madam! May blessings, wealth, and good fortune be yours!" When Bhikshus seek alms, they stand silently and accept whatever offerings are given. If none are offered, they simply leave, without becoming upset. That's how mendicant monks differ from ordinary beggars.

The second meaning of "Bhikshu" is "frightener of demons." Because a Bhikshu is very proper and upright, the demons from the heavens and the externalists are afraid of him. The demons and ghosts stay far away from him. His proper energy overcomes all deviant beings.

The third meaning is "destroyer of evil." Ordinary

people find it difficult to give up their bad habits. Bhikshus who cultivate the Way, however, concentrate on giving up bad habits and reforming themselves. They are able to make a new start, changing their faults and becoming good. That's why they are called destroyers of evil.

Present in the assembly were eight thousand great Bhikshus **and thirty-six thousand Bodhisattvas Mahā-sattvas.** Bodhisattva is a Sanskrit word, but it has become a very popular term in China. Although many people use it, most don't know what it really means. "A Bodhisattva is just a Bodhisattva!" they say.

A "Bodhisattva" is a sage of the Great Vehicle. The full Chinese transliteration of the Sanskrit term is *putisaduo*, but the Chinese use the abbreviated form *pusa*. "Bodhisattva" means "one who enlightens sentient beings." Bodhisattvas are one of the nine Dharma Realms of living beings and also one of the Four Dharma Realms of Sages. A Bodhisattva uses his enlightened wisdom to rescue and liberate all sentient beings, beings with blood and breath. Although beings without blood and breath, such as plants, are considered insentient, they do have natures, and they are born and grow within the Buddhas' great, bright, light treasury.

A Bodhisattva is also defined as "an enlightened sentient being." The Bodhisattva is the same as other living beings, except that he is enlightened. Being enlightened, he "does no evil and practices all good deeds." He has no bad habits or faults. Having attained supreme wisdom, he is not confused anymore, so he does not act out of ignorance.

Ordinary living beings always bungle things up in their ignorance. They don't have any real wisdom. When confronted with a problem, they don't know how to handle it, because they are unenlightened. Those of the Two Vehicles are self-enlightened—they have come to understanding and are no longer confused. However, they have not tried to teach other people the method by which they themselves became enlightened. Bodhisattvas are enlightened themselves, and they also share their enlightened wisdom with other living beings, teaching those beings to become enlightened through the method they themselves used. Bodhisattvas enlighten themselves and also enlighten others, but their enlightenment is not complete. A Buddha is one who has enlightened himself, enlightens others, and perfected his enlightened practice. Since he is perfect in the three enlightenments and replete with the myriad virtues he is called a Buddha.

When Bodhisattvas continue to advance, they can attain Buddhahood. There are many different levels of Bodhisattvahood; for example, there are Bodhisattvas of the First, Second, Third, Fourth, Fifth, Sixth, Seventh, Eighth, Ninth, and Tenth Grounds. When Tenth Ground Bodhisattvas reach the level of Equal Enlightenment, their enlightenment is virtually equal to that of the Buddhas—they are only one step away from Buddhahood.

"Mahāsattvas" are great Bodhisattvas endowed with great vows, great wisdom, and great skill and accomplishment in cultivation. There were thirty-six thousand of such Bodhisattvas in the assembly of Medicine Master Buddha, which was as vast as the ocean.

Also kings, ministers. Various kings were also present. Kings rule the country in order to bring blessings and prosperity to the people, and they are assisted by ministers.

Brahmans. The Brahmans [the priestly class] were one of the two noble classes in ancient India. While practicing, Brahmans, like Buddhists, may observe certain ascetic practices and be vegetarian, their goal is to be born in the heavens. Although they cultivate purity and asceticism, they do not work on subduing greed, anger, and delusion. Their equivalent in China is the Taoists. Despite their external differences, Brahmans and Taoists share similar practices and beliefs. There are quite a few skilled cultivators among the Brahmans.

Lay disciples. While others may address you by the title of "Upasaka" or "Upasika" [titles for a Buddhist layman and laywoman, respectively] it is not permissible to use these titles to refer to yourself. Some laypeople print business cards giving their names as "Upasaka So-and-so," and they also speak of themselves as Upasakas. Such people do not know the proper etiquette. Maybe you don't understand what I mean, so let me talk about "Mr." instead. In China, *xiansheng* ("Mr.") is the most common form of address. Other people may address you as "Mr. So-and-so" out of respect, but you certainly wouldn't introduce yourself as "Mr. Smith" or "Mr. Jones." If you shamelessly call yourself *xiansheng*, you simply don't understand the Chinese language. This is something everyone should know. Remember not to call yourself "Mr. Smith" or "Upasaka Smith." "Mr." is a title reserved for learned, virtuous elders, and "Upasaka" is used for a layman who has ten kinds of virtue.

"Dharma Master" is also a title used by others to address you. If you call yourself a Dharma Master, you are praising yourself. It's like calling yourself the emperor.

Others can hail the emperor, "Long live your Majesty!" but the emperor does not say that to himself. That's common sense. The same goes for the title "Upasaka" and "Dharma Master." These are respectful forms of address. You use them to respect others, not yourself. Of course you should respect yourself, but you don't need to make a show of it. The lore and knowledge of Chinese culture is boundless and inexhaustible. If you miss one small point, you may end up making a big blunder. These rules of etiquette are commonly overlooked.

There were also **gods, dragons, and the rest of the eightfold division**. Our temple is protected by the gods, dragons, and the rest of the eightfold division of ghosts and spirits. You may all remember that when we first moved into Gold Wheel Monastery and began renovating it, some people saw a vision of Guanyin Bodhisattva sitting in mid-air with his foot resting on a tortoise. On the eastern corner of the property, there used to be a bar where drug dealers, winos, strippers, and other disreputable people would hang out. Then, just before our opening ceremony, the bar was closed down for good. It used to be a bad neighborhood, but now it's much cleaner. This is a response from the gods, dragons, and the rest of the eightfold division, who protect the monastery.

When this place was a church, some rather messy people came and left food all over the ground, attracting a lot of mice. We are now propagating the Buddhadharma here, so the gods, dragons, and the rest of the eightfold division should protect this temple and quickly chase the mice away. Actually, I wouldn't really mind the rats, except that they give people the impression that our place is very unsanitary. So now we request the Dharma-protecting spirits to do their job and protect this monastery. Chase away the mice and any other beings that should not be here. Don't be polite with them.

The eightfold division is comprised of the gods, dragons, *yakṣas, gandharvas, asuras, garuḍas, kinnaras,* and *mahoragas.*

The gods in the heavens made vows in the past to protect the Buddhas' temples.

Dragons are magical beings. When they cultivated in past lives, they were "fast with the Vehicle and slow with the precepts." They practiced Great Vehicle (Mahāyāna) Buddhism with tremendous vigor. Seeking a shortcut to obtaining spiritual powers, they practiced esoteric dharmas with intensity, but neglected to hold the precepts. They weren't careful to abstain from evil and practice good. For their esoteric practices, sometimes they would steal skulls from corpses and recite mantras over them. They would also steal the plaques that people put up to honor their ancestors, and then they would command ghosts and spirits using those ancestors as mediums.

Dragons were cultivators who advanced at a rocket-like speed, but who didn't pay much attention to the precepts. They casually broke the precepts against sexual misconduct, lying, killing, and stealing. They stole human skulls and ancestral plaques, and even the trees growing by people's graves, in order to carry out their practices. They approached the Dharma with crooked, greedy minds. That's how they were "fast with the Vehicle and slow with the precepts." Because they were fast with the Vehicle, they have spiritual powers when they become dragons.

Because they were slow with the precepts, they fell into the animal realm.

Dragons are animals, but they are also spiritual creatures. Through its spiritual powers, a dragon has the ability to change size at will from the very small to the very large and can also suddenly vanish and just as suddenly reappear. However, dragons have a great fear of the sun because when they bake in the sun, it's as painful as being scorched by fire. They have to send down some rain to soak themselves—just like taking a shower. These are the dragons that dwell in the heavens.

Yakṣas are called "speedy ghosts" because they travel very quickly. There are space-travelling *yakṣa*, ground-travelling *yakṣas*, and water-travelling *yakṣas*. They travel faster than cars, airplanes, and even rockets. They can travel ten thousand miles in a single thought. There are a great variety of *yakṣas*, just as there are great varieties of dragons: golden dragons, fire dragons, green dragons, white dragons, black dragons, and so on. There are also many ethnic groups in the human race, and within each ethnic group or nationality, there are further distinctions of southerners, northerners, easterners, and westerners. All these different groups of people have their own languages and writing systems. In general, countless species of living beings populate the world, and each species contains infinite variations within it. That's the wonder of the world.

People will never completely understand the secrets of the world. Now with people going to the moon, it seems we are about to experience a breakthrough and everything will be understood. However, when everything is understood, the world will come to an end. When everything has been discovered, it will all disappear. The play will be over! Once people on earth can communicate with and travel to other planets, the world's population will be wiped out by nuclear weapons, or by natural disasters such as earthquakes and volcanic eruptions. No matter how flourishing the world becomes, when it reaches the height of its glory, it will become dark again, just as day turns into night. We rise in the morning and begin the day; and when the day is over, we go to sleep. As soon as we close our eyes, we become muddled and unclear. All things, great and small, in the world, go through cycles.

Gandharvas are spirits that make delightful music. When they play their music in the heavens, the immortals sit there totally enraptured, oblivious to the passing of time. However, *gandharvas* won't play their music for just anyone. The Jade Emperor can enjoy their music, because he knows their weakness. He knows that once they get a whiff of incense, they immediately come wanting to sniff it, no matter how many tens of thousands of miles away they might be. The Jade Emperor has a special kind of incense that he uses to attract them. When they arrive at his palace and smell the incense, they start dancing and singing. That is why *gandharvas* are called "incense-inhaling spirits." There are eight dragon kings, and four *gandharva* kings.

There are four kinds of *asuras*. *Asuras* have huge tempers. They are always getting angry. People who have big tempers are controlled by *asuras*. In the heavens, *asuras* are called "those without wine" since they have no wine to drink. They are also known as "non-gods" because their status in the heavens is like that of illegal aliens in America, who live in America and can enjoy American bread and butter, but who cannot vote or run for office. The *asuras* in the heavens are constantly at war with Lord Shakra's heavenly troops, hoping to overthrow Shakra *[the Jade Emperor]* and usurp his throne. They can live in the heavens and enjoy the blessings of the gods, but they do not have any authority there.

Garuḍas are the great golden-winged Peng birds. They also have the ability to grow large or small, and to appear and disappear at will. Their wingspan is 330 *yojanas.* One *yojana* is 40 miles long, so you can see how long 330 *yojanas* must be! With one flap of its wings, a Peng bird dries up the waters of the sea so that it can gobble up all the exposed dragons—big, little, young, and old! With another flap of its wings, it can level the mountains by moving them into the ocean.

Garuḍas have very great spiritual penetrations, and dragons used to fear them more than anything. But since the *garuḍas* have taken refuge with the Buddha, they live in peace with the dragons and don't eat them anymore. Chapter One of the *Wonderful Dharma Lotus Flower Sutra* explains the four kinds of *garuḍas.*

Kinnaras are called "doubtful spirits," because they look like humans, except that they have a single horn growing on top of their heads. They also make extremely fine music.

Mahoragas are spirits of huge pythons. The gods, dragons, and the rest of the eightfold division include former demons, ghosts, and goblins who reformed and became Dharma-protectors of Buddhism. So you see, bad people sometimes turn around and become good. As it is said, "The sea of suffering is boundless; a turn of the head is the other shore." Those who committed the ten evil deeds or the five rebellious acts can still start anew and become good. Since the ghosts and spirits of the eightfold division felt bad about the harm they had done to Buddhism before, they vowed to protect Buddhism.

There were also **beings human and non-human.** People came to protect the Buddha's teaching and support the Triple Jewel, and so did other kinds of beings.

The immeasurable great multitude respectfully surrounded him, and he spoke Dharma for them. The countless beings in the Dharma assembly respectfully surrounded the Buddha as he spoke the Dharma.

Sutra:

> At that time, the Dharma Prince Mañjuśrī, receiving the awesome inspiration of the Buddha, rose from his seat, bared one of his shoulders, knelt on his right knee, and, inclining his head and placing his palms together, said to the Bhagavan, "World Honored One! We wish you would speak about such Dharmas as the Buddhas' names, the great vows they made in the past, and their supreme merit and virtue, so that those who hear them will be rid of their karmic hindrances. This request is also for the sake of bringing benefit and joy to sentient beings in the Dharma Image Age."

Commentary:

At that time, the Dharma Prince Mañjuśrī. The Buddha is the Dharma King, and the Bodhisattvas are Dharma Princes. Since Mañjuśrī, as a Bodhisattva of Equal Enlightenment, is due to achieve Buddhahood very soon, he is called a Dharma Prince, the son of the Dharma King. **Receiving the awesome inspiration of the Buddha.** He respectfully received the awesome spiritual power of the Buddhas of the ten directions and **rose from his seat.**

He **bared one of his shoulders.** He uncovered his right shoulder. Why did he do this? First of all, it was a custom in India, where the weather is extremely warm, for people to expose their right shoulders in order to let the hot air escape from under their clothes. In this way they could keep themselves cool. Secondly, uncovering the right shoulder is a way to show respect for the Buddha. When one uncovers the right shoulder, one is according with worldly conventions on the one hand and seeking the transcendental Dharma on the other. The real and the conventional are mutually inseparable and do not obstruct each other.

Mañjuśrī Bodhisattva **knelt on his right knee, and, inclining his head and placing his palms together, said to the Bhagavan**—the World Honored One. This represents respect in both body and mind and the purity of the three karmas.

"World Honored One! We wish you would speak about such Dharmas... All of us in the Dharma assembly are of one mind right now. We all hope the Buddha will speak of such dharmas **as the Buddhas' names,** the names of Medicine Master Vaiḍūrya Light Tathāgata and the Buddhas in the ten directions, **the great vows they made in the past, and their supreme merit and virtue.** Please tell us how they amassed such supreme merit and virtue when they were practicing the Bodhisattva Way.

"...so that those who hear them will be rid of their

karmic hindrances. When living beings hear of the Buddhas' vows and of their merit and virtue, offenses and karmic hindrances will disappear and they will return to purity!

"This request is also for the sake of bringing benefit and joy to sentient beings in the Dharma Image Age. We wish all living beings to be free from worry and suffering." In the Dharma-Image Age, people will build many temples and Buddha images, but there will be very few real cultivators. Mañjuśrī Bodhisattva is requesting the Buddha to speak Dharma for those in the assembly, as well as for people in the Dharma Image and Dharma Ending Ages.

Sutra:

> The Buddha then praised the Pure Youth Mañjuśrī: "Good indeed! Good indeed, Mañjuśrī. With great compassion you now request that I speak about the Buddhas' names and the merit and virtue of their past vows, for the sake of rescuing sentient beings who are bound up by karmic obstacles, and for the purpose of bringing benefit, peace, and joy to beings who live in the Dharma Image Age. Listen attentively to my words and reflect on them extremely well, for I will now answer you."
>
> Mañjuśrī said, "Please do speak. We are glad to listen."

Commentary:

The Buddha then praised the Pure Youth Mañjuśrī. Mañjuśrī Bodhisattva had begun practicing the Bodhisattva Way as a virgin youth, and he eventually became the foremost leader among Bodhisattvas. The Buddha praised him, saying, "**Good indeed! Good indeed, Mañjuśrī.** You are a fine Bodhisattva. You are a terrific Bodhisattva! I am praising you because **with great compassion you now request that I speak.** You have a heart of great kindness and compassion. Such kindness can gather in those who lack affinities. You are now requesting the Dharma for the sake of all living beings, whether or not they have affinities. Compassionately wishing to save all beings, you ask me to tell everyone **about the Buddhas' names and the merit and virtue of their past vows.**

"**For the sake of rescuing sentient beings who are bound up by karmic obstacles,** who are suffering in the three evil paths, **and for the purpose of bringing benefit, peace, and joy to beings who live in the Dharma Image Age,** you are requesting the Dharma. You wish to benefit all the sentient beings in the Dharma Image Age, causing them to be happy and free from afflictions.

"**Listen attentively to my words and reflect on them extremely well, for I will now answer you.** Listen well and reflect carefully on the Dharma that I will now explain to you."

Mañjuśrī said, "**Please do speak. We are glad to listen.** Buddha, please be compassionate and speak for us. We all now wish to hear the Buddha explain this Dharma."

Sutra:

> The Buddha told Mañjuśrī, "**Passing from here to the east, beyond Buddhalands numerous as the sand grains in ten Ganges rivers, is a world called 'Pure Vaiḍūrya.' The Buddha there is named Medicine**

Master Vaiḍūrya Light Tathāgata, Of Proper and Equal Enlightenment, Perfect in Understanding and Practice, Well Gone One, One Who Understands the World, Supreme Lord, Regulating Hero, Teacher of Gods and Humans, Buddha, Bhagavan. Mañjuśrī, when that World Honored One, Medicine Master Vaiḍūrya Light Tathāgata, was practicing the Bodhisattva path in the past, he made twelve great vows that enable all sentient beings to obtain what they seek."

Commentary:

The Buddha told Mañjuśrī, "Passing from here to the east, beyond Buddhalands numerous as the sand grains in ten Ganges rivers, is a world called 'Pure Vaiḍūrya.' If you start from our Sahā world and go east, passing over Buddhalands as many as the sand grains in ten Ganges rivers, or perhaps even more than that number, you will reach a world called the Pure Vaiḍūrya Land. That world is translucent and pure, and the ground is made of Vaiḍūrya.

The Buddha there is named Medicine Master Vaiḍūrya Light Tathāgata. Like all Buddhas, he has the ten titles. **Of Proper and Equal Enlightenment, Perfect in Understanding and Practice.** He has already realized the Unsurpassed, Proper, Equal and Right Enlightenment. His cultivation and wisdom are both perfected. **Well Gone One, One Who Understands the World.** He is the wisest person in the world; his understanding is unsurpassed. **Supreme Lord; Regulating Hero, Teacher of Gods and Humans, Buddha, Bhagavan.** "Bhagavan" means "World Honored One."

"**Mañjuśrī, when that World Honored One, Medicine**

Master Vaiḍūrya Light Tathāgata, was practicing the Bodhisattva path in the past, before he became a Buddha, he made twelve great vows. People who cultivate should make real vows. We should bring forth genuine, great vows from our hearts, and then we should practice according to them. Medicine Master Tathāgata made twelve great vows that enable all sentient beings to obtain what they seek.

Our cultivation is relatively easy, compared to Śākyamuni Buddha's. Śākyamuni Buddha cultivated for three great *asaṅkhyeyas* of eons before becoming a Buddha. An *asaṅkhyeya* is an uncountable number. Medicine Master Buddha also cultivated the Bodhisattva path for many *asaṅkhyeyas* of eons before realizing Buddhahood. Now we can rely on the vows made by the Buddhas. We are the Buddhas' disciples, and they have bequeathed to us the Three Treasuries and Twelve Divisions of the Canon. But can we accept this legacy of supreme Dharma treasures? If we want to be true disciples of the Buddha, then the legacy is ours. However, if our merit and virtue are insufficient and we don't want to be true sons of the Buddha, then we cannot inherit this legacy.

Because of Medicine Master Buddha's twelve great vows, sentient beings can obtain whatever they seek and soon become Buddhas. Through the vows of past Buddhas, we can realize a great fruition with just a little bit of effort. We should be overjoyed to encounter this Dharma, and we should advance vigorously in our practice!

Sutra:

"The first great vow: 'I vow that in a future life, when

63

I attain *anuttarasamyaksaṁbodhi,* my body will shine with dazzling light that will illumine measureless, countless, boundless worlds. My body will be adorned with the thirty-two heroic features and the eighty subsidiary characteristics, and I will enable all beings to become as I am.'

"The second great vow: 'I vow that in a future life when I attain Bodhi, my body will be as bright and clear as *vaiḍūrya,* flawlessly pure, vastly radiant, majestic with merit and virtue, abiding at ease, adorned with blazing nets brighter than the sun and the moon. Beings dwelling in darkness will be illuminated and will succeed in all their endeavors.'"

Commentary:

Every Buddha and Bodhisattva, before achieving Buddhahood, makes infinitely many great vows to benefit and help living beings. When he becomes a Buddha, his vows come true, and, like a magnet, they attract living beings from the ten directions. If his vows are great, then the power of the magnet is great, and no matter how many living beings there are and how heavy their karmic obstacles are, his vows can draw them in. Living beings, despite their ignorance, can sense that he wishes to help them, and so they feel especially close to him. Deep down in their souls they intuitively sense this affinity. In the past, Medicine King Bodhisattva burned his body and gave up his life as an offering to the Buddhas. We, in contrast, can't even bear to burn a finger, let alone our whole bodies.

The first great vow: "I vow that in a future life, when I attain *anuttarasamyaksaṁbodhi*—the Unsurpassed, Proper and Equal, Right Enlightenment—**my body will shine with dazzling light that will illumine measureless, countless, boundless worlds."** This is the very first great vow that Medicine Master Tathāgata made.

"My body will be adorned with the thirty-two heroic features and the eighty subsidiary characteristics of a Buddha, **and I will enable all beings to become as I am.** I will benefit all sentient beings, causing them to have bodies just like mine, with light that shines on infinitely many worlds. I don't want to be the only one who becomes a Buddha and illuminates living beings; I want all the living beings illuminated by me to have bodies just like mine." Because Medicine Master Buddha made such a vow, all of us who are listening to the Sutra have the opportunity to attain bodies like his. You shouldn't look down on yourself, saying, "I wouldn't want to shine with dazzling light. What good is it?" Well, what's so good about not having such dazzling light?

The second great vow: "I vow that in a future life when I attain Bodhi, my body will be as bright and clear as *vaiḍūrya,* **flawlessly pure, vastly radiant, majestic with merit and virtue, abiding at ease, adorned with blazing nets brighter than the sun and the moon.** When I become a Buddha, my body will be as clear and transparent as *vaiḍūrya,* free of blemishes and defilements. Its light will be indescribably brilliant. It will have a commanding appearance, and its merits and virtues will be so numerous that one cannot see them all at once. My body will be comfortable and free of sickness, and will be surrounded by fiery nets of light that outshine the sun and moon. **Beings dwelling in darkness will be illuminated** by its light, **and**

will succeed in all their endeavors. They will accomplish whatever task or calling they undertake." See how considerate the Buddha is! In benefiting beings, he doesn't forget a single detail. In fact, no one cares for us more than the Buddha. He is our closest friend and relative.

Sutra:

"The third great vow: 'I vow that in a future life when I attain Bodhi, I will, by means of limitless, unbounded wisdom and skill-in-means, enable all sentient beings to obtain an inexhaustible supply of material necessities so they are without the slightest want.'"

Commentary:

The third great vow. Medicine Master Buddha made this vow in his past lives when he was still cultivating as a Bhikshu; he was no different from you, me, and other living beings then. But because he made great vows, he was able to achieve Buddhahood very quickly. We still haven't become Buddhas, because we are too selfish, greedy, and quarrelsome, and we don't want to make great vows.

I vow that in a future life when I attain Bodhi, I will, by means of limitless, unbounded wisdom and skill-in-means. Medicine Master Buddha uses wise expedients, not stupid ones, to teach and transform living beings. While wise expedients may not necessarily benefit oneself, they benefit others. Wise expedients are wholesome and in accord with Dharma. Stupid expedients are unwholesome and go against the Dharma.

What are unwholesome expedients? Doing wrong things and then rationalizing them as "expedient." For example, someone may rationalize the killing of a mosquito as an expedient, saying that it doesn't violate the precept against killing. Someone else might justify stealing something that doesn't belong to him, saying, "I'm just being expedient! What difference does it make whether he uses it or I use it? We're all the same." However, stealing is not in accord with Dharma; it's an evil deed. As for sexual misconduct, a man may know very well that his extramarital affair will upset his wife, but he thinks, "Why should I worry about her? I'm just being expedient, that's all!" He thinks sexual misconduct is an "expedient dharma." All people know how to defend their infidelity. They know it's wrong, yet they still say it doesn't matter. Do they really know then? People rationalize lying and taking intoxicants as well.

"I think I'll have a little wine, just for the fun of it. What's wrong with that? I'm not getting drunk or anything!"

"Why should I be worried about telling a little lie? It's not like I'm committing a murder. What's the big deal?"

Expedients can be wise or stupid. Stupid expedients are wrong deeds that people rationalize as "expedient." Medicine Master Vaiḍūrya Light Tathāgata uses wise expedients.

He does this to **enable all sentient beings to obtain an inexhaustible supply of material necessities so they are without the slightest want.** See how generous the Buddha's heart is! He provides living beings with everything they need and fulfills all their wishes. If you are greedy, learn to recite this Buddha's name or this Sutra, quick! Then you'll be able to satisfy your greed!

"I know," you say, "I'll recite Medicine Master Buddha's

name with the wish of winning a few million dollars at the casinos in Reno." If you are sincere, your wish might come true. But if you waver between faith and doubt, you can't fool the Buddha.

Sutra:

"The fourth great vow: 'I vow that in a future life when I attain Bodhi, I shall lead those sentient beings who practice deviant paths to reside in the Way of Bodhi, and those who travel on the vehicles of the Hearer or Pratyekabuddha to abide in the Great Vehicle.'"

Commentary:

In **the fourth great vow,** Medicine Master Buddha wants to cause deviant beings to become proper, confused beings to become enlightened, and those in suffering to find bliss. He also wishes that adherents of the Small Vehicle will study and practice the Great Vehicle, resolve their minds on Bodhi, and realize Buddhahood. So he said, **"I vow that in a future life when I attain Bodhi,** when I become a Buddha and attain Proper and Equal, Right Enlightenment, **I shall lead those sentient beings who practice deviant paths to reside in the Way of Bodhi."** Very few people possess proper understanding, while many have deviant understanding. If you expound the Proper Dharma, very few people can understand, accept, and put it into practice. On the other hand, if you teach heterodox theories, esoteric dharmas, or "shortcut" dharmas, people, with their deeply ingrained deviant views, are immediately eager to learn. "Deviant paths" refers to casting hexes, poisoning people, consulting oracles, or communicating with spirits through mediums. Such dharmas are very popular. If you lecture on the Sutras in the proper manner, people find it boring and uninteresting. But if you make deviant prophecies, such as, "A disaster is about to befall you. If you want to save yourself, you'd better do as I tell you!" then people listen.

Although they practice deviant paths, Medicine Master Buddha sets up expedient methods to help them wake up from confusion and establish proper views, so that they can "reside in the Way of Bodhi." To reside there means to renounce deviant teachings, develop wisdom, end birth and death, and dwell in enlightenment. Wise people practice the Proper Dharma while stupid people walk a narrow, external path. To reside in the Way of Bodhi means to leave the external sects and go over to genuine Buddhism.

And those who travel on the vehicles of the Hearer or Pratyekabuddha. Hearers cultivate the Dharma of the Four Noble Truths, which are suffering, accumulation, cessation, and the Way. Pratyekabuddhas (also known as Those Enlightened to Conditions) cultivate the Twelve Conditioned Causes, which are as follows:

1. ignorance, which (is the condition that) brings on
2. activity, which brings on
3. consciousness, which brings on
4. name and form, which bring on
5. the six entrances, which bring on
6. contact, which brings on
7. feeling, which brings on
8. craving, which brings on
9. grasping, which brings on

10. becoming, which brings on

11. birth, which brings on

12. old age and death

The twelve conditioned causes describe the process by which all living beings come into and pass out of existence. As it is said, "All activities are impermanent, subject to production and extinction. When production and extinction are extinguished, that still extinction is bliss." If one understands the Twelve Conditioned Causes, then one can wake up from confusion and cultivate the Six Perfections of the Great Vehicle.

The Twelve Conditioned Causes

We were born from *ignorance*. Ignorance is the root of birth and death, the source of all troubles and afflictions. The goal of our practice is to break through ignorance. Ignorance confuses us, so that we live as if drunk or dreaming, driven by the desires for wealth, sex, fame, food, and sleep. Ignorance causes us a lot of trouble. Once there is ignorance, it manifests in *activity*. We act on what we don't understand, and then we become attached to appearances. When *consciousness* arises and begins to discriminate, the marks of self, others, living beings, and a life span appear. Activity and consciousness bring *name and form* into being, so that we can talk about things. Then the whole body comes into being, and with it, the *six entrances* [eyes, ears, nose, tongue, body, and mind]. The six entrances come into *contact* with the external environment, and that contact brings on *feeling*. We differentiate between good and bad sensations, trying to avoid unpleasant sensations while craving pleasant ones. Thus, feeling then brings on *craving*. As we grasp at the object of our craving, there is *becoming*, then *birth* into the next life, and then *old age and death* all over again. The Twelve Conditioned Causes describe the endless rounds of rebirth that all living beings undergo.

Pratyekabuddhas feel that this cycle is a lot of suffering, so they practice the Way in order to liberate themselves from birth and death. When they succeed, they attain to the fruition and become Pratyekabuddhas or Solitarily Enlightened Ones, who belong to one of the Two Vehicles.

The Two Vehicles consist of the Hearers and Those Enlightened to Conditions (also called Solitarily Enlightened Ones). The term "vehicle" is used to designate a class of cultivators. The practice of the Two Vehicles is not ultimate, because they have ended only physical birth and death, not the birth and death of thoughts. This is why Medicine Master Buddha vowed to lead the cultivators of the Small Vehicle **to abide in the Great Vehicle** and to resolve their minds on realizing the Buddhas' Unsurpassed Enlightenment.

Sutra:

"The fifth great vow: 'I vow that in a future life when I attain Bodhi, I shall enable limitless and boundless numbers of sentient beings who cultivate Brahma conduct within my Dharma to perfectly uphold the three clusters of precepts without exception. Should there be any violation, upon hearing my name, they will regain their purity and not fall into the evil destinies.'"

Commentary:

The name of Medicine Master Vaiḍūrya Light Tathāgata has saved many of us from falling into the three evil paths. If this Buddha's name didn't exist in the world, all of us might have fallen into the hells, turned into hungry ghosts, or become animals long ago, and it would be very difficult for us to become humans again. But because of Medicine Master Buddha's vows, even if you have committed the ten evils, or broken the precepts or the rules of pure eating, if you hear this Buddha's name with its myriad virtues, you will attain bliss and be freed from offenses, suffering, and birth and death.

Medicine Master Buddha knows that since most living beings do not uphold the precepts, their karma is a mixture of good and evil. It's like a muddy puddle in which dirt and water are mixed. Water represents wisdom, and dirt ignorance. By upholding the precepts, one can return to the origin and discover one's inherent wisdom. Not upholding the precepts is like muddying the clear water of wisdom with the dirt of ignorance. However, upholding the precepts is not an easy thing to do.

Because Medicine Master Buddha knew that living beings have many bad habits and faults and are prone to make mistakes, he made **the fifth great vow,** saying: **I vow that in a future life when I attain Bodhi,** when I become a Buddha, **I shall enable limitless and boundless numbers of sentient beings,** which includes you and me, **who cultivate Brahma conduct within my Dharma to perfectly uphold the three clusters of precepts without exception.** Brahma conduct refers to pure conduct, to the strict observance of the precepts. Medicine Master Buddha vows that whoever practices the Buddhadharma will be able to perfectly uphold the pure precepts. Pure upholding of precepts can be compared to a perfectly round, full moon.

The Three Clusters of Pure Precepts:
1. The precepts for gathering in living beings
2. The precepts comprised of wholesome dharmas
3. The precepts comprised of the rules of discipline and deportment

Since it's not easy for people to uphold the precepts, Medicine Master Buddha vowed, **"Should there be any violation, upon hearing my name, they will regain their purity.** In the event of having violated the precepts, if one hears my Buddha-name, one will return to the origin **and not fall into the evil destinies.** One will not fall into the hells, the realm of hungry ghosts, or the animal realm."

In the "three clusters of pure precepts," each cluster is a collection of many precepts. Just as there are said to be "three hundred rituals and three thousand modes of awesome deportment," the precepts comprised of the rules of discipline and deportment are also a large collection of rules.

Wholesome dharmas refers to innumerably many kinds of dharmas. The precepts comprised of wholesome dharmas tell us to "do no evil and practice all good." The precepts for gathering in living beings encompass all living beings. One wants to take all living beings across to Buddhahood. The three clusters of precepts are very many and therefore not easy to cultivate. What should we do if we accidentally transgress them? Medicine Master Buddha's vow says, "If sentient beings transgress the precepts, after they hear my name, they will attain purity. They won't fall into the evil destinies."

Think it over. Medicine Master Buddha works so hard to gather in living beings. Shouldn't we acknowledge his compassion? Shouldn't we cultivate the precepts seriously and stop relying on his aid? Don't think, "Medicine Master Buddha has vowed to save me even if I violate the precepts, so I don't have to worry." If we violate a precept unintentionally, without realizing it, he can help us regain purity. On the other hand, we cannot violate the precepts on purpose and think that the Buddha will save us.

Sutra:

"The sixth great vow: 'I vow that in a future life when I attain Bodhi, if there are sentient beings whose bodies are inferior and whose faculties are imperfect, who are ugly, dull, blind, deaf, mute, deformed, paralyzed, hunchbacked, or afflicted with skin disease, insanity, or various other sicknesses and sufferings, upon hearing my name they shall all become endowed with upright features, keen intelligence, and perfect faculties, and they shall be free of sickness and suffering.'"

Commentary:

The sixth great vow: "I vow that in a future life..." Some people don't believe in future lives. If there were no future lives, then you could commit murder and do whatever you wanted. But since there are future lives, and consequences for everything you do, you cannot misbehave and do as you please.

74

"Why don't I know anything about my past or future lives?" you ask. Well, when you sleep, do you know about the things that happen when you're awake? No. In the same way, in this life you have forgotten about the events of your past lives. That's why the Buddha said, "If you want to know what you did in previous lives, take a look at what you're undergoing now. If you want to know what your future lives will be like, take a look at what you're doing now." The karma you create in this life will certainly come to fruition in the future.

Because the Buddha was aware of this, he vowed, "In a future life **when I attain Bodhi,** when I attain the Unsurpassed, Proper and Equal, Right Enlightenment, **if there are sentient beings whose bodies are inferior,** whose features are distorted... Perhaps their eyes, ears, and nose are squeezed close together, or their mouth grows where the ears should be.

"I've never seen anyone who looked like that," you say. No? Well, you shouldn't think of trying to become like that, either. There are many people who are born looking like dogs, cats, mice, bears, horses, deer, and so on. They're a frightful sight.

And whose faculties are imperfect. They may have only one eye, one ear, or one nostril. Some of their features may be mutilated or deformed. Perhaps some of their limbs and faculties don't function normally, so that even though they are in the right place, they don't serve any use.

The text elaborates on those "whose bodies are inferior and whose faculties are imperfect," describing them as those **who are ugly,** not good-looking, or **dull,** not intelligent. They're very slow. If you try to teach them that two plus two is four, they say, "What? One plus two is three. How did you get four?" The **blind** have eyes, but cannot see. The **deaf** have ears, but cannot hear. When **mutes** try to talk, their voice stays down in their throat and they are no louder than a mosquito. They are basically incapable of speech. How miserable it is to be blind, deaf, or mute! People undergo such retributions because, in the past, they doubted the Dharma and didn't like to listen to it. Since they came face to face with the Buddha and didn't recognize him, they became blind. They didn't listen when people tried to speak Dharma to them, so they became deaf. They stubbornly refused to study the Dharma, so they became mute.

Deformed, paralyzed, hunchbacked. People whose joints or limbs are deformed may not be able to extend them. Hunchbacks look as if a round-bottomed cooking-pot were stuck on their back, or as if they had the hump of a camel.

Or afflicted with skin disease. Skin disease disfigures people in various ways, perhaps covering their faces with patches of different colors. Those suffering from **insanity** include severely abused children, who may bite themselves or try to eat their own fingers. People undergo the retribution of skin disease, insanity, **or various other sicknesses and sufferings** because they slandered the Mahāyāna Sutras, such as the *Śūraṅgama Sūtra*, or disparaged the Buddha's teachings in the past.

Upon hearing my name, "Medicine Master Vaiḍūrya Light Tathāgata," **they shall all become endowed with upright features, keen intelligence, and perfect faculties, and they shall be free of sickness and suffering.** Ugly and dull people will become attractive and intelligent, and their eyes, ears, noses, tongues, bodies, and minds will become fully functional. All sickness and pain will disappear even though they haven't taken medicine or seen a doctor. Isn't this wonderful? All we have to do is hear the name of Medicine Master Buddha. See how much this Buddha wants to help us? He doesn't want us to suffer our karmic retributions, and he wishes to grant our wishes and make us truly happy.

Sutra:

"The seventh great vow: 'I vow that in a future life when I attain Bodhi, I shall cause sentient beings who are oppressed by many illnesses and who are without aid, without a place to turn, without a doctor, without medicine, without relatives, and without a family, who are poverty-stricken and filled with suffering to be cured of their sicknesses upon having my name pass by their ear, so they are peaceful and happy in body and mind. They will have a family and relatives, and acquire an abundance of property and wealth, and even realize unsurpassed Bodhi.'"

Commentary:

Many of the newcomers still don't know who Medicine Master Vaiḍūrya Light Tathāgata is. I shall tell you a little more about this Buddha. He is a great king of physicians who cures people without using medicine. Living beings only need to hear his name, and their illnesses will be cured.

Chinese physicians use the methods of looking, listening, asking, and feeling the pulse to diagnose a patient's condition. Physicians are classified as "spiritual," "sagely," "skillful," or "clever." The "spiritual" are the very best, while the "sagely" are not quite as good. "Skillful" refers to those who have to apply some skill and effort before they can know a person's condition. The "clever" can know in an ingenious way. In general, the "spiritual" know by looking; the "sagely" know by listening; the "skillful" know through asking; and the "clever" know through feeling the pulse. Ordinary doctors must use these four methods to diagnose sickness.

Medicine Master Buddha, however, doesn't use these methods. He can cure people as long as they sincerely recite his name. That's his special way of helping people. Such awesome spiritual power comes from the following vow.

The seventh great vow: "I vow that in a future life when I attain Bodhi, I shall cause sentient beings who are oppressed by many illnesses, and who are without aid, without a place to turn, without a doctor, without medicine, without relatives, and without a family, who are poverty-stricken and filled with suffering. They have no one who can help them, and no safe place where they can take refuge. Being sick is the greatest suffering. They're poor and alone and beset by hardships.

To be cured of their sicknesses upon having my name pass by their ear. If they hear my name, "Medicine Master Buddha Who Quells Disasters and Lengthens Life," they will be cured of all disease, without having to take medication or get shots, X-rays, or CAT scans. There's no need for electrotherapy, acupuncture, or any other treatments or operations. However, this passage doesn't mean that doctors will be out of business, so doctors should not worry!

So they are peaceful and happy in body and mind. They will have a family and relatives, and acquire an abundance of property and wealth. They will fully regain physical and mental health. They will not be alone in the world, nor will they be poor.

And finally, they will **even realize unsurpassed Bodhi**. All living beings have the Buddha-nature and can become Buddhas. The Buddha didn't say, "I alone can become a Buddha, and no one else can." Buddhism is very democratic. The Buddha is just the same as us, except that he has great wisdom, so he doesn't say or do confused things. We study the Buddha's teachings in order to learn to live in harmony, be good people, and ultimately, become wise Buddhas. However, if we do not behave properly, we will never become wise.

Sutra:

> "The eighth great vow: 'I vow that in a future life when I attain Bodhi, if there are women who give rise to a deep loathing for their female body and wish to renounce it because they are oppressed and disturbed by the myriad sufferings of being female, upon hearing my name, they will be able to turn from women into men who are replete with male features and ultimately realize unsurpassed Bodhi.'"

Commentary:

Why would women want to become men? Don't misunderstand and think that Buddhism considers women to be bad. Some members of the Women's Lib movement in America have accused Amitābha Buddha of being a male chauvinist, because his Land of Ultimate Bliss is "men only." Actually, Amitābha Buddha doesn't discriminate between "men" or "women." Why does his Buddhaland have no women? It's because it is a Pure Land, and the bodies of women are sometimes impure.

Some people prefer not to be women, because they don't want to undergo the myriad sufferings of being female. There are extremely many sufferings, not a fixed number. The myriad sufferings refer to the many troublesome pains and sicknesses that commonly afflict women. Their bodies are periodically unclean, and during those times, they cannot do much.

When a woman has her menstrual period, she's usually not in a good mood. Some women experience great pain right before or after their periods. Their menstruation may be irregular, so that it doesn't stop flowing, or else they never have their period. These problems make having a woman's body very inconvenient, and so some cultivators prefer to be men.

Moreover, the sexual desire between men and women can be very strong. In this day and age, there are all sorts of strange problems. Demons and ghosts take advantage of the lust between men and women and stir up trouble, especially when it comes to homosexuality.

In **the eighth great vow,** Medicine Master Buddha says: **"I vow that in a future life when I attain Bodhi,** when I become a Buddha, **if there are women who give rise to a deep loathing for their female body and wish to renounce it because they are oppressed and disturbed by the myriad sufferings of being female,** if they desperately wish to renounce the bodies of women, **upon hearing my** name, they will be able to turn from women into men who are replete with male features and ultimately realize unsurpassed Bodhi. They will become just like men, and will eventually attain the supreme fruit of Buddhahood."

Sutra:

"The ninth great vow: 'I vow that in a future life when I attain Bodhi, I shall liberate sentient beings from the nets of demons and the bonds of external sects. If they have fallen into the dense forests of evil views, I shall lead them to have proper views and to gradually cultivate the practices of Bodhisattvas so they will quickly realize unsurpassed, proper and equal Bodhi.'"

Commentary:

The ninth great vow concerns destroying the nets of demons and gaining liberation from the dense forests of the evil views of externalists. Medicine Master Buddha said: "**I vow that in a future life when I attain Bodhi, I shall free sentient beings from the nets of demons.**" Right now as people, we are very close to the demons and very far from the Buddhas. If we wish to be a demon, we can do so anytime. If we wish to become Buddhas, we have to break through many dense forests of evil views. We have to cast out deviant views and constantly cultivate proper views before we can escape the demons' nets. As these nets are very tough to break, we may easily become followers of demons and *asuras.* If we are always getting angry or doing stupid things, we are in the demons' nets.

When a fisherman nets a big fish, he thinks, "What a big fish I've caught for supper today!" When a demon catches a person in its net, it thinks, "Great! I've got another person for my retinue!" How can we escape the nets of demons? It's very simple. Just avoid getting mad and doing stupid things. Demons use their tricks to lead people to believe in wrong views, and it's very difficult for them to get free. However, if we rely on the power of Medicine Master Buddha's vow, it becomes very easy to escape the demons' nets.

And the bonds of external sects. External sects follow the demons in the heavens. They use various methods to control people, even making them swear that if they disobey, they will be struck by lightning or suffer other calamities. Thus the adherents of external sects dare not offer any opposition, even though they know their belief is mistaken. They have no freedom and cannot escape.

If they have fallen into the dense forests of evil views. There are all sorts of deviant knowledge and views, as thick as forests, that totally control people's minds. Buddhism, however, does not attempt to control people. I once announced to a group of Buddhists in the presence of the Roman Catholic Cardinal of Taiwan, Paul Yubin, "If you think Buddhism is too old-fashioned and you want to find a new, trendy religion, here is your chance to change your faith. Buddhism is not a prison. People are free to choose whatever religion they like." Then I turned to Cardinal Yubin, "Do you dare to tell your followers the same thing?" He couldn't do it, because his religion still wants to control people. Those who desert the religion are considered the greatest offenders. The "dense forests of evil views" refers to views that cannot be brought out into the open and discussed in public.

Medicine Master Buddha says, "When I meet people of deviant views, **I shall lead them to have proper views and to gradually cultivate the practices of Bodhisattvas.** I shall explain proper views to them and teach them to cultivate the Six Perfections and myriad practices of Bodhisattvas **so they will quickly realize unsurpassed, proper and equal Bodhi.**"

Sutra:

> "The tenth great vow: 'I vow that in a future life when I attain Bodhi, I shall cause sentient beings who fall into the hands of the law and are bound, interrogated, whipped, fettered, imprisoned, sentenced to execution, or subjected to endless disasters, hardships, abuse, and humiliation so that they are torn by grief and distress and suffering in body and mind, to obtain, upon hearing my name, liberation from all worry and suffering by means of my blessings, virtue, and awesome spiritual power.'"

Commentary:

The tenth great vow: "I vow that in a future life when I attain Bodhi, I shall cause sentient beings who fall into the hands of the law and are bound, interrogated, whipped, fettered, imprisoned, sentenced to execution, or subjected to endless disasters, hardships, abuse, and humiliation so that they are torn by grief and distress and suffering in body and mind..." People may be arrested on false charges, or they may break the law by accident and end up in prison. They are interrogated, and later their own testimony is used to incriminate them. They are flogged, beaten, and bound hand and foot, losing their freedom and being cut off from the outside world. Under the mental and physical anguish, they feel as if they were being roasted alive. Perhaps they are sentenced to die, because the government wants to make an example out of them—they may be beheaded, shot, or electrocuted.

To obtain, upon hearing my name, liberation from all worry and suffering by means of my blessings, virtue, and awesome spiritual power. Medicine Master Buddha vowed, "If such people hear my Buddha-name, then by means of the blessings and virtue that I cultivated in past lives, they will be saved from all disasters and hardships, and will obtain bliss."

Sutra:

> "The eleventh great vow: 'I vow that in a future life when I attain Bodhi, I shall cause all sentient beings who are so plagued by hunger and thirst that they create all kinds of bad karma in their quest for food, upon hearing my name and single-mindedly accepting and maintaining it, to be filled with delicious food and drink and afterward, by means of the flavor of Dharma, to settle in ultimate peace and happiness.'"

Commentary:

The eleventh great vow: "I vow that in a future life when I attain Bodhi, I shall cause all sentient beings who are so plagued by hunger and thirst—either because they have no food or drink at all, or because they are unable to eat and drink what they have—that they create all kinds of bad karma in their quest for food." Their hunger may drive them to plunder and kill in order to obtain food and drink.

Medicine Master Buddha vowed, "Upon hearing my name and single-mindedly accepting and maintaining it... If they retain my name in their minds, I will cause them to be filled with delicious food and drink. I will make appear all kinds of delicious food so that they may eat their fill; and afterward, by means of the flavor of Dharma, I will cause them to settle in ultimate peace and happiness. Then I will explain the Dharma to them, so that they may taste its supreme, wonderful flavor and attain perfect peace and bliss."

Sutra:

"The twelfth great vow: 'I vow that in a future life when I attain Bodhi, if there are sentient beings who are poor and without clothes so that day and night they are troubled by mosquitoes and flies, and by cold and heat, upon hearing my name and single-mindedly accepting and maintaining it, they shall obtain all kinds of fine and wonderful garments that accord with their tastes, as well as a variety of precious adornments, flower garlands, fragrant balms, and the enjoyments of music and various kinds of talents, so that all their hearts' delights will be fulfilled.'"

Commentary:

Medicine Master Buddha must have known poverty and hardship in the past, and so he made vows to save all living beings from such suffering. In the twelfth great vow, he says, "I vow that in a future life when I attain Bodhi, if there are sentient beings of any nationality or ethnic background, who are poor and without clothes. The previous vow was to save beings without food, but this vow talks about beings who have neither food nor clothes, so that day and night they are troubled by mosquitoes and flies, stinging and biting insects, and by cold and heat. Without clothes, they suffer day and night from the cold and the heat. Upon hearing my name, the name I will have as a Buddha, and single-mindedly accepting and maintaining it. That's the main thing—you have to single-mindedly recite the name. Bringing the mind to one, you recite Medicine Master Buddha's name in thought after thought, all day long.

They shall obtain all kinds of fine and wonderful garments that accord with their tastes. They obtain the most wonderful clothing, exactly the kind they like, as well as a variety of precious adornments, playthings made of the seven treasures—gold, silver, *vaiḍūrya*, crystal, mother of pearl, red pearls, and agate. They obtain whatever catches their fancy, for example, flower garlands made of the seven treasures, expensive fragrant balms to give as offerings to the Buddhas, and the enjoyments of music and various kinds of talents, so that all their hearts' delights will be fulfilled. They obtain all these playthings for their amusement.

Sutra:

"Mañjuśrī, these are the twelve sublime and wonderful vows that the World Honored One, Medicine Master Vaiḍūrya Light Tathāgata, One of Proper and

Equal Enlightenment, made while cultivating the Bodhisattva Way."

Commentary:

Sākyamuni Buddha calls out to the wisest of Bodhisattvas, **Mañjuśrī,** whose name means "Wonderfully Auspicious." (His Bodhimaṇḍa is on China's Mount Wutai, which is snow-covered all year round. He probably chose Mount Wutai because he likes to cultivate in cold places.) Sākyamuni Buddha addresses this wise Bodhisattva, Mañjuśrī, because only a very wise person can understand the great vows of Medicine Master Vaiḍūrya Light Tathāgata.

These are the twelve sublime and wonderful vows that the World Honored One, Medicine Master Vaiḍūrya Light Tathāgata, One of Proper and Equal Enlightenment, made while cultivating the Bodhisattva Way. "World Honored One" and "One of Proper and Equal Enlightenment" are two of the ten titles of Buddhas. Although twelve vows are not very many, these vows can solve the problems of all living beings, whether they are suffering or happy, wise or ignorant. The vows are called "sublime" because they are extremely important and can rescue all beings.

Sutra:

"Moreover, Mañjuśrī, if I were to speak for an eon or more about the great vows made by the World Honored One, Medicine Master Vaiḍūrya Light Tathāgata, when he practiced the Bodhisattva Way and about the merit, virtue, and adornments of his Buddhaland, I could not finish."

Commentary:

"**Moreover, Mañjuśrī,**" Sākyamuni Buddha continues. "**If I were to speak for an eon or more about the great vows made by the World Honored One, Medicine Master Vaiḍūrya Light Tathāgata, when he practiced the Bodhisattva Way and about the merit, virtue, and adornments of his Buddhaland,** the Vaiḍūrya Land in the East, **I could not finish.** Even if I spoke continuously for a great eon or more, I still could not finish in that long a time."

Sutra:

> "**That Buddhaland has always been completely pure; there are no women, no evil destinies, and no sounds of suffering. The ground is made of *vaiḍūrya*, with golden cords lining the roads. The city walls, towers, palace pavilions, studios, windows, and latticework are all made of the seven treasures. The merit, virtue, and adornments of this land are identical to those of the Western Land of Ultimate Bliss.**"

Commentary:

That Buddhaland has always been completely pure. It is always clean, pure, and undefiled, as bright and clear as *vaiḍūrya*. **There are no women** in the Vaiḍūrya Land. Some women's rights activists object to Amitābha Buddha's Land of Ultimate Bliss, saying, "Why are there no women in that land? Does Amitābha Buddha look down on women? Does he favor men over women?" Not at all. We should realize that the Sahā world, in which men and women engage in lust, is filled with all kinds of evil and suffering. There is nothing worthwhile here. Everything is unclean.

The Sahā world is known as the World of the Five Turbidities. Our time is very impure—that's the *turbidity of the eon*. The things we see with our eyes are also unclean—that's the *turbidity of views*. We all have incredibly many afflictions—that's the *turbidity of afflictions*. Living beings are all born from emotional desire, and they are differentiated into males and females—that's the *turbidity of living beings*. Not only human beings, but all beings with blood and breath are this way—born from sexual desire and dying from sexual desire. Even germs are imperceptibly brought into existence by this kind of desire. As long as there is desire, one is impure. The *turbidity of life* comes about because beings in the Sahā world live in an extremely unclean environment. The things we see, hear, smell, taste, touch, and think about are all unclean. Thus, this is known as the Evil World of the Five Turbidities.

In contrast to our dusty, defiled world, there is no dirt in the heavens; nor in the Western Land of Ultimate Bliss, where the ground is paved with gold; nor in the Eastern Vaiḍūrya Land, which has ground made of Vaiḍūrya.

The people in the Land of Ultimate Bliss are born transformationally from the vows of Amitābha Buddha, and they are free of desire. The Vaiḍūrya Land is created from the vows of Medicine Master Buddha. Because these Buddha lands are completely free of desire and birth occurs by transformation, not by sexual reproduction, there are no women in these lands.

No evil destinies and no sounds of suffering. The hells, hungry ghosts, and animals do not exist in the

89

Vaiḍūrya Land. There aren't any heart-breaking sounds of pain, sorrow, or distress.

The ground is made of *vaiḍūrya,* **with golden cords lining the roads.** The Vaiḍūrya Land is so named because its ground is made of Vaiḍūrya. Ropes and railings made of gold are used to mark the sides of the roads.

The city walls overlook the moat of the city. **Towers** are lookout towers above the city gate, or openings in the city wall. **Palace pavilions** refers to two-story buildings inside the palace.

Studios refer to individual rooms. The **windows** are clear, and everything is very clean. **And latticework.** There are seven rows of trees and seven layers of netting. They **are all made of the seven treasures**—gold, silver, *vaiḍūrya,* crystal, mother of pearl, red pearls, and agate.

The merit, virtue, and adornments of this land are identical to those of the Western Land of Ultimate Bliss. They are exactly the same. As the saying goes, "Akṣobhya in the East, Amitābha in the West." Akṣobhya (Medicine Master) Buddha, the teaching host of the Vaiḍūrya Land, leads the Vajra Division. Amitābha Buddha, the host of the Land of Ultimate Bliss, leads the Lotus Division.

At the City of Ten Thousand Buddhas, we recite the name of Medicine Master Buddha in the morning and dedicate the merit to the Dharma-protectors of the City, praying that they will be safe from disasters and will enjoy long life. At noon we recite "Namo Fundamental Teacher Śākyamuni Buddha" in order to repay the kindness of Śākyamuni Buddha, who taught the Dharma to us. In the evening we recite the name of Amitābha Buddha, vowing to be born in the Land of Ultimate Bliss, where the three evil paths do not exist. In the Sahā world, we are troubled and afflicted every day, but in the Land of Ultimate Bliss and the Vaiḍūrya Land, there is only happiness.

The City of Ten Thousand Buddhas is a new Way-place, and we recite the names of three different Buddhas in the morning, at noon, and in the evening. In this respect, we differ from Way-places in China, Hong Kong, Taiwan, Singapore, Vietnam, and other countries where they follow the Chinese Buddhist tradition and recite Amitābha Buddha's name all the time. When left-home people from other places visit the City of Ten Thousand Buddhas, they think that we do everything wrong and do not understand the rules.

We do not claim that what we do at the City of Ten Thousand Buddhas is correct. However, when we rise in the morning, we should emulate the vows of Medicine Master Buddha Who Quells Disasters and Lengthens Life. This will give us the fresh, youthful energy of dawn; an invigorating vitality like that of trees reviving after a drought or a spring bubbling forth from the ground. When we rise at dawn, the fire of our life burns brightly and everything is auspicious. At noon, we should be grateful to Sākyamuni Buddha for all the Dharma and Sutras that he taught us. At night, our thoughts return to the Land of Ultimate Bliss, the final haven where we wish to be reborn.

All these years, you assumed that other places did things the same way. You didn't realize that the City of Ten Thousand Buddhas has a different style. For example, at all of the monasteries of Dharma Realm Buddhist Association, we begin each Sutra lecture with a formal requesting of Dharma. You won't see this at other temples. I am telling you this because you are not familiar enough with the Buddhist rituals to know if it is right or not.

Does anyone have questions, criticisms, or opinions on this passage of the Sutra or on my explanation of it? In studying the Dharma, we should investigate the principles until we are completely convinced of them, without the slightest doubt in our minds. If you disagree with something in the Sutra, speak up.

If you really have no deluded thoughts, then you have already been born in the Land of Ultimate Bliss. If you are truly free of desire, then you have already taught and transformed living beings. Who told you to indulge in deluded thoughts? Who told you to have thoughts of desire? If no one told you, then it's empty and false. If someone told you, who was it? If it was you, then why weren't you aware of it when the deluded thought first arose in your mind?

Your not having any deluded thoughts is already the Pure Land. See how convenient, how immediate it is! Simply clean up your deluded thoughts, and you'll be in the Land of Ultimate Bliss. When you have no deluded thoughts, then you have no afflictions. That freedom from afflictions, that happiness, is itself the Land of Ultimate Bliss. So, don't go running all over the place!

The Pure Land teaches very clearly, "One definitely creates it; one doesn't really go anywhere." You create the Pure Land yourself by revealing the light of your own nature.

The Pure Land is in the mind.
Amitābha is in one's own nature.

You needn't look outside. Ordinary people think that the Pure Land is outside, but if you really want to study and cultivate Buddhism, you must understand that the Land of Ultimate Bliss and the Sahā world are not beyond this very thought. A defiled thought is the Sahā world, while a pure thought is the Land of Ultimate Bliss.

Don't be attached to the fact of your teaching living beings or being reborn in the Land of Ultimate Bliss. Recite the Buddha's name without worrying about whether you will be reborn there. Just cultivate sincerely. If you are free of affliction, then the Land of Ultimate Bliss is right here, ready-made. If you become afflicted, then you are in the Sahā world, with its unspeakable suffering.

Sutra:

"Residing in that land are two Bodhisattvas Mahā-sattvas; the first is called Universally Radiant Sunlight, and the second, Universally Radiant Moonlight. They are the leaders among the immeasurable, uncountable hosts of Bodhisattvas in that land and will be the successors to that Buddha. They are able to maintain the precious treasury of the Proper Dharma of the World Honored One, Medicine Master Vaidūrya Light Tathāgata. Therefore, Mañjuśrī, all good men and women who have faith should vow to be born in that Buddha's land."

Commentary:

Residing in that land are two Bodhisattvas Mahāsattvas. Sākyamuni Buddha said there is no distinction between Medicine Master Tathāgata and Amitābha Tathāgata, or between their respective Buddhalands. Now he speaks of two great Bodhisattvas in the Vaiḍūrya Land. **The first is called Universally Radiant Sunlight, and the second, Universally Radiant Moonlight. They are the leaders among the immeasurable, uncountable hosts of Bodhisattvas in that land and will be the successors to that Buddha.** These two Bodhisattvas assist Medicine Master Buddha in teaching the beings of the Vaiḍūrya Land. When Medicine Master Buddha retires from the Buddha-position, Universally Radiant Sunlight Bodhisattva will take his place; and when he in turn retires, Universally Radiant Moonlight Bodhisattva will fill the position.

They are able to maintain the precious treasury of the Proper Dharma of the World Honored One, Medicine Master Vaiḍūrya Light Tathāgata. After these two Bodhisattvas become Buddhas, they will continue to honor the vows made by Medicine Master Buddha, adorning themselves with that Buddha's merit, virtue, and adornments and using his methods to teach beings. They will receive and uphold Medicine Master Vaiḍūrya Light Tathāgata's vows and practices, thereby maintaining the precious treasury of the Proper Dharma.

Therefore, Mañjuśrī, all good men and women who have faith should vow to be born in that Buddha's land so that they can meet Medicine Master Vaiḍūrya Light Tathāgata and eventually become Buddhas themselves.

Sutra:

> **At that time, the World Honored One again spoke to the Pure Youth Mañjuśrī saying, "Mañjuśrī, there are living beings who don't distinguish good from evil,**

who indulge in greed and stinginess, and who know nothing of giving or its rewards. They are stupid, ignorant, and lack the foundation of faith. They accumulate much wealth and many treasures and ardently guard them. When they see a beggar coming, they feel displeased. When they have to practice an act of charity that does not benefit themselves, they feel as though they were cutting a piece of flesh from their body, and they suffer deep and painful regret.

"There are other innumerable avaricious and miserly living beings who hoard money and necessities that they don't use even for themselves, how much less for their parents, wives, or servants, or for beggars! At the end of their lives, such beings will be reborn among the hungry ghosts or animals. If they heard the name of that Buddha, Medicine Master Vaiḍūrya Light Tathāgata, in their former human existence, and they recall that Tathāgata's name for the briefest moment while they are in the evil destinies, they will immediately be reborn in the human realm. Moreover, they will remember their past lives and will dread the sufferings of the evil destinies. They will not delight in worldly pleasures, but will rejoice in giving and praise others who give. They will not begrudge giving whatever they have. Gradually, to those who come to beg, they will be able to give away their own head, eyes, hands, feet, and even their entire body, to say nothing of their money and property!"

Commentary:

At that time, the World Honored One, Sākyamuni

Buddha, **again** compassionately **spoke to the Pure Youth Mañjuśrī, saying, "Mañjuśrī, there are living beings who don't distinguish good from evil,** who mix up good and evil, **who indulge in greed and stinginess,** unable to give things away, **and who know nothing of giving or its rewards.** They don't know how to be generous or how to treat people well. They don't understand that they should give to the needy.

There are three kinds of giving:

1. The giving of wealth
2. The giving of Dharma
3. The giving of courage

The giving of wealth means giving away one's wealth and property, including one's skills and talents, to help other people. In giving Dharma, one bestows teachings suited to the needs of each individual, like a physician prescribing medicine. When one sees people who are suffering or in danger, one may bestow courage by comforting them and dispelling their fears. These are the three kinds of giving. If you have no wealth, you can give Dharma. If you have no Dharma, then you can give courage. You may also explain the rewards of giving to others, telling them, for example, that in giving one thing, one may reap a reward ten thousand times greater (as stated in Chapter Ten of the *Earth Store Sutra*).

They are stupid, ignorant, and lack the foundation of faith. Ignorant people are those who have never heard the principles of cause, effect, and retribution. Those who lack faith and wisdom are skeptical when they hear the Proper Dharma. They do not have Dharma-selecting vision—the wisdom to determine the truth. They take what is true to be false, and vice versa.

They accumulate much wealth and many treasures and ardently guard them. There are misers in this world, who think about their wealth and treasures twenty-four hours a day. How they exhaust themselves! They are so preoccupied with guarding their riches that they can't taste their food or get a wink of sleep! Wouldn't you call that suffering?

When they see a beggar coming, they feel displeased. They think, "How dare you beg from me, you despicable thing!" **When they have to practice an act of charity that does not benefit themselves...** Perhaps they are compelled by circumstances to give to charity. If they don't give, there will be trouble. When they are forced to give in this way, **they feel as though they were cutting a piece of flesh from their body, and they suffer deep and painful regret.** For them, giving money is just like cutting the flesh from their body. The pain sears their hearts, and they cannot bear to do it.

There are other innumerable avaricious and miserly living beings who hoard money and necessities that they don't use even for themselves, how much less for their parents, wives, or servants, or for beggars! There are countlessly many "stingy ghosts" who amass riches and store them away, not allowing anyone to use them. They cannot even bear to use these things themselves, so how could they possibly let their parents or wives enjoy them? How much less would they share their wealth with servants or beggars!

At the end of their lives, such beings will be reborn

among the hungry ghosts or animals. Such misers may turn into poor ghosts, hungry ghosts, money-guarding ghosts, or animals.

If they heard the name of that Buddha, Medicine Master Vaiḍūrya Light Tathāgata, in their former human existence, and they recall that Tathāgata's name for the briefest moment while they are in the evil destinies, they will immediately be reborn in the human realm. As humans, they might have heard someone reciting the name of Medicine Master Buddha. If they remember that Buddha's name while they are in the three evil paths, they will be reborn in the human realm. **Moreover, they will remember their past lives.** Having the knowledge of past lives, they **will dread the sufferings of the evil destinies. They will not delight in worldly pleasures, but will rejoice in giving and praise others who give.** They will no longer indulge in eating, drinking, and making merry, but will instead delight in giving to all living beings and will praise those who do charity.

No longer misers, they will not begrudge giving whatever they have. Gradually, to those who come to beg, they will be able to give away their own head, eyes, hands, feet, and even their entire body to anyone who seeks for them, **to say nothing of their money and property!** How much more will they be able to renounce other possessions!

By giving, one reaps blessings. Those who were stingy in past lives are poor now, while those who were generous are now rich. It is said, "You must first give in order to get something in return. If you don't give, you won't get anything." We must be clear about cause and effect. If you

make even a tiny mistake in cause and effect, the consequences may be terrible. When we come to the temple to
bow to the Buddhas, we should try to benefit others, not
try to gain something for ourselves. We should be willing
to take a loss. People who come to the temple to steal food,
money, or other things will certainly fall into the three
evil paths.

Be sure to tell your relatives and friends that, no matter
what temple they go to, they shouldn't go there hoping to
obtain responses or bargains, or to steal things. If they do,
they are creating great offenses. If you fail to tell them, then
you have a share in their offenses. You should clearly
explain the law of cause and effect to them, so they won't
make mistakes.

The Sutras tell us to give to others, not to constantly be
seeking offerings from others. Buddhists should benefit
others. Otherwise, we will only be "thieves among the
virtuous." If we constantly exploit situations and pull
strings with the Dharma-protectors, we are simply creating
offenses and trying to destroy Buddhism.

Hearing my advice, I hope you will wake up and
quickly take stock of yourself! If you have faults, change
them right away; and if you don't, then try even harder to
be a good Buddhist. Don't be a phony Buddhist who tries
to take advantage of Buddhism. Don't be tempted to do
business within Buddhism, for it will surely lead you to the
hells! The woman who came to our temple and tried to sell
jewelry didn't realize that she was asking for a terrible
retribution. Be extremely careful. If you fall, I won't be able
to save you.

Sutra:

"Moreover, Mañjuśrī, there are beings who, although they study under the Tathāgata, nonetheless violate the *śīla*. Others, although they do not violate the *śīla*, nonetheless transgress the rules and regulations. Others, although they do not violate the *śīla* or rules and regulations, nonetheless destroy their own proper views. Others, although they do not destroy their own proper views, nonetheless neglect learning, so they are unable to understand the profound meaning of the Sutras that the Buddha speaks. Others, although they are learned, nonetheless give rise to overweening pride. Shadowed by overweening pride, they justify themselves and disparage others, slander the Proper Dharma, and join the retinue of demons.

"Such fools act on their misguided views and further, cause immeasurable millions of beings to fall into pits of great danger. These beings will drift endlessly in the realms of the hells, the animals, and the ghosts. But if they hear the name of Medicine Master Vaiḍūrya Light Tathāgata, they will be able to renounce their evil practices and cultivate wholesome Dharmas, and thereby avoid falling into the evil destinies. If those who have fallen into the evil destinies because they could not renounce their evil practices and cultivate wholesome Dharmas, by the awesome power of the past vows of that Tathāgata, get to hear his name for only a moment, then after they pass out of that existence, they will be reborn again as human beings. They will hold proper views and will be ever vigorous. Their minds will be well-regulated and joyful, enabling them to renounce their families and leave the householder's life. They will take up and maintain study of the Tathāgata's Dharma without any violation. They will have proper views and erudition; they will understand profound meanings and yet be free from overweening pride. They will not slander the Proper Dharma and will never join the ranks of demons. They will progressively cultivate the practices of Bodhisattvas and will soon bring them to perfection."

Commentary:

"Moreover, Mañjuśrī..." Sākyamuni Buddha, in his great compassion, feared that living beings would not heed Medicine Master Buddha's instructions or his awesome spiritual power. Fearing that this wonderful Dharma would go in one ear and out the other, that we wouldn't really hear it, he wanted to explain it in more detail for those of us in the Dharma-Ending Age.

He said, **"There are beings who, although they study** the Dharma **under the Tathāgata, nonetheless violate the** *śīla*." *Śīla* is Sanskrit and refers to moral precepts that guard against evil and wrongdoing. Some people do not guard against wrongdoing, but recklessly break the precepts.

Others, although they do not violate the *śīla*, **nonetheless transgress the rules and regulations** that everyone should honor and abide by. **Others, although they do not violate the** *śīla* **or rules and regulations, nonetheless**

destroy their own proper views. Such people abide by the rules, and yet are influenced by improper views. They have a strange manner and a peculiar point of view.

Others, although they do not destroy their own proper views, nonetheless neglect learning. They are lazy when it comes to studying the Dharma. They waste time and pass up the opportunity to study the *prajñā*-wisdom in the Sutras, **so they are unable to understand the profound meaning of the Sutras that the Buddha speaks.** They have no wish to comprehend the truths in the Sutras, which "tally with the principles of the Buddhas above and the potentials of living beings below." Instead, they treat the Sutras as their enemies.

Others, although they are learned, nonetheless give rise to overweening pride. Some people have neither broken the precepts and rules, nor destroyed their proper views, nor neglected to study. But because they are erudite and have studied many Sutras, they become arrogant and think they are better than everyone else.

Shadowed by overweening pride, they justify themselves and disparage others. With their wisdom obstructed by their arrogance, they justify themselves and denounce others. They **slander** monasteries where people practice **the Proper Dharma**, criticizing such practices as eating one meal a day, not lying down to sleep, and not keeping money. They say no one should cultivate in the Dharma Ending Age. Really! I wonder what sort of Buddhism they study!

And join the retinue of demons. Such people become the friends and followers of demons. **Such fools act on their misguided views,** behaving improperly **and further,**

cause immeasurable millions of beings to fall into pits of great danger, from which they cannot escape. These beings will drift endlessly in the realms of the hells, the animals, and the ghosts, undergoing endless suffering.

But if they hear the name of Medicine Master Vaiḍūrya Light Tathāgata... If these beings, who have committed the ten unpardonable offenses (*pārājika*), the ten evils, or the five rebellious acts—offenses that merit falling into the Relentless Hells—get to hear that Buddha's name, they will be able to renounce their evil practices, which were based on improper views, and cultivate wholesome Dharmas, and thereby avoid falling into the evil destinies. Then they will not fall into the hells or among the hungry ghosts, animals, or *asuras*.

If those who have fallen into the evil destinies because they could not renounce their evil practices and cultivate wholesome Dharmas... Some beings may not be able to renounce their evil deeds right away and cultivate precepts, erudition, and proper views. They also find it difficult to follow the rules and regulations. However, if, by the awesome power of the past vows of that Tathāgata, they get to hear his name for only a moment, then after they pass out of that existence, they will be reborn again as human beings. The Buddha manifests before those beings and, using various expedients, causes them to hear the name of Medicine Master Vaiḍūrya Light Tathāgata so that when they die, they will be reborn as human beings.

Once reborn as human beings, they will hold proper views and will be ever vigorous. Their minds will be well-regulated and joyful, enabling them to renounce their families and leave the householder's life. They are always happy, because they avoid selfishness, pursuing self-benefit, fighting, greed, and seeking, knowing that these are causes for falling. They see through the transient affairs of the world and leave home to cultivate the Way.

They will take up and maintain study of the Tathā-gata's Dharma without any violation. They will have proper views and erudition; they will understand pro-found meanings and yet be free from overweening pride. They will vigorously study the Dharma under Medicine Master Vaiḍūrya Light Tathāgata. Never again will they transgress the precepts or rules, destroy their own proper views, or become lazy in their studies. Although they grasp the most profound and subtle principles in the Sutras, they will not become arrogant. **They will not slander the Proper Dharma and will never join the ranks of demons.** They do not join the demons' retinue. **They will progressively cultivate the practices of Bodhisattvas and soon bring them to perfection.** Cultivating the Bodhisattva practices step by step, they will soon realize perfect enlightenment.

Sutra:

"Moreover, Mañjuśrī, if there are sentient beings who harbor stinginess, greed, and jealousy, who praise themselves and disparage others, they will fall into the three evil destinies for countless thousands of years where they will undergo intense suffering. After under-going intense suffering, at the end of their lives they will be born in the world as oxen, horses, camels, and donkeys that are constantly beaten, afflicted by thirst and hunger, and made to carry heavy burdens along the roads. Or they may be reborn among lowly people, as slaves or servants who are always ordered around by others and who never for a moment feel at ease.

"If such beings, in their former lives as humans, heard the name of the World Honored One, Medicine Master Vaiḍūrya Light Tathāgata, and by this good cause are able to remember it and sincerely take refuge with that Buddha, then, by means of the Buddha's spiritual power, they will be liberated from all sufferings. They will be endowed with keen faculties, and they will be wise and erudite. They will always seek the supreme Dharmas and encounter good friends. They will eternally sever the nets of demons and smash the shell of ignorance. They will dry up the river of afflictions and be liberated from birth, old age, sickness, death, anxiety, grief, suffering, and vexation."

Commentary:

Śākyamuni Buddha patiently calls out again, **"Moreover, Mañjuśrī, if there are sentient beings who harbor stinginess, greed, and jealousy..."** A stingy person is a miser, but works like a dog to save up money for his children and grandchildren. Some people are insatiable; they are greedy even for garbage, thinking they can convert it into energy. Jealous people try to hinder others from obtaining benefit. People may be jealous of others' talents, intelligence, blessings, happy lives, or good fortune. Usually, jealousy is hidden in the mind, and is not seen by others until it manifests in one's behavior.

The Bodhisattva Precepts speak very clearly about those

105

who praise themselves and disparage others. Actually, people have sharp eyes. If you are truly good, they will be able to tell. You don't have to say anything. But some people advertise themselves, "Hey, do you know who I am? I'm a great Bodhisattva. I'm enlightened. I have great spiritual powers." They praise themselves, but criticize everyone else, including the Buddha! They say God is unfair and Mother Earth is unkind. As for such people, I tell you, **they will fall into the three evil destinies for countless thousands of years where they will undergo intense suffering.** It's not known how many eons they will suffer as hell-beings, hungry ghosts, and animals. By praising themselves and slandering others, and by being stingy, greedy, and jealous, they use up every last bit of virtue and blessings and so must suffer all sorts of unbearable pain.

After undergoing intense suffering, at the end of their lives they will be born in the world not as humans, but **as oxen, horses, camels, and donkeys that are constantly beaten, afflicted by thirst and hunger, and made to carry heavy burdens along the roads.** As beasts of burden, they toil under oppressive conditions, constantly being flogged and often going without food and water. They never know a moment of happiness.

Or they may be reborn among lowly people, as slaves or servants who are always ordered around by others and who never for a moment feel at ease. When they are nearly finished paying for their offenses, they become people again, but are born into the poorest families, where they do not have adequate food, clothes, or shelter. They may also become slaves or servants, who must take orders from others and are never at ease.

If such beings, in their former lives as humans, heard the name of the World Honored One, Medicine Master Vaiḍūrya Light Tathāgata, and by this good cause—this good seed, are able to remember it and sincerely take refuge with that Buddha... In this life they may once again think of that Buddha's name and take refuge in him with utmost sincerity. Then, by means of the Buddha's awesome spiritual power, by the spiritual power of his great vows, they will be liberated from all sufferings and distress. They will be endowed with keen faculties. They will have excellent seeing, hearing, and a highly developed sense of smell. They will have discerning taste buds. They will have an acute sense of touch, and will be very intelligent with good memories.

And they will be wise and erudite, understanding many principles. They will always seek the supreme Dharmas. Not being satisfied with small achievements, they will always strive to advance. They won't grow weary and quit. When living beings with good roots encounter Medicine Master Vaiḍūrya Light Tathāgata, they will not be lazy. And they will always encounter good friends and good advisors who help them.

They will eternally sever the nets of demons. They will be liberated from the demon king's retinue forever, and will not be caught in their nets. And they will smash the shell of ignorance. For people who study Buddhism, it is crucial to smash the shell of ignorance. Ignorance is like an eggshell that isolates you. Inside the shell, you have no idea of what is going on outside. Being all confused inside that shell of ignorance, you start having idle thoughts that lead to doing something wrong.

They will dry up the river of afflictions and be liberated from birth, old age, sickness, death, anxiety, grief, suffering, and vexation. They will leave all these problems behind, and always dwell in the four virtues of Nirvana—permanence, bliss, true self, and purity.

Fundamentally, our tempers do not come from the food we eat, nor from heaven or earth, nor from the weather. They come from our own ignorance. Ignorance comes from selfishness, as do afflictions, indirectly. We have so much anger and affliction simply because we are afraid to suffer a loss. Not wanting to take a loss, we get mad and fight. If we did not fight, were not greedy, did not seek anything, were not selfish, and did not want to benefit ourselves, we would have no anger.

Among the Bodhisattvas, Guanyin Bodhisattva has great compassion, and if you recite his name, he will relieve your suffering and pain. He has great affinities with all beings. If you wish to strengthen your ties with Guanyin Bodhisattva, recite his name more often and let your light blend with his.

Earth Store Bodhisattva has great vows. He cannot bear to see any living being in suffering. If we recite his name, he will help us to quickly attain Buddhahood with his awesome spiritual power. Did these two Bodhisattvas place advertisements in the Sutras to promote themselves? No. The Buddha, who always speaks the truth, personally praised them and told us about their great compassion and great vows.

Sutra:

"Moreover, Mañjuśrī, there may be beings who delight in perversity and engage in legal disputes, bringing trouble to others as well as themselves. In their actions, speech, and thoughts, they create ever-increasing amounts of evil karma. Never willing to benefit and forgive others, they scheme to harm one another instead. They pray to the spirits of the mountain forests, trees, and graves. They kill living beings in order to make sacrifices of blood and flesh to the *yakṣa* and *rākṣasa* ghosts. They write down the names of their enemies and make images of them, and then they hex those names and images with evil mantras. They summon paralysis ghosts, cast hexes, or command corpse-raising ghosts to kill or injure their enemies.

"However, if the victims hear the name of Medicine Master Vaiḍūrya Light Tathāgata, then all those evil things will lose their power to do harm. The evildoers will become kind to one another. They will attain benefit, peace, and happiness and no longer cherish thoughts of malice, affliction, or enmity. Everyone will rejoice and feel content with what they have. Instead of encroaching upon each other, they will seek to benefit one another."

Commentary:

This passage shows how the proper overcomes the deviant and how the true destroys the false. Śākyamuni Buddha says, **Moreover, Mañjuśrī,** let me explain for you in greater detail. **There may be beings who delight in perversity.** Such beings deny truth, confounding right and wrong.

They stir up trouble for no reason and use false principles to bully the powerless.

And engage in legal disputes. They file suits and take people to court. Although the court is supposed to uphold justice, they use their illogical arguments to convince the court to rule their defendant innocent. That's how they invert right and wrong and cover up the truth. If they lose their case, they appeal to a higher court. They're determined to fight, and they won't give up until they die!

Bringing trouble to others as well as themselves, not allowing themselves or others a moment of peace, **in their actions, speech, and thoughts, they create ever-increasing amounts of evil karma.** Their bodies kill, steal, and engage in sexual misconduct. Greed, anger, and delusion fill their minds. Their mouths utter harsh speech, lies, frivolous speech, and duplicity. As they commit these Ten Evil Deeds with increasing frequency, their offenses become more and more serious.

Never willing to benefit and forgive others, they scheme to harm one another instead. Involved in endless, vengeful feuds, they are unable to forgive and forget past wrongs, and unwilling to benefit others under any circumstances. In their schemes of harming others, they even resort to the aid of ghosts and spirits. **They pray to the spirits of the mountain forests, trees, and graves.** They bow to mountain spirits, earth deities, animal spirits, and just about everything else, even "dung and urine" spirits! Since they are themselves filthy, they bow to filthy spirits.

They pray to spirits, and to the lonely souls and desolate ghosts in the graves, saying, "If you protect me and kill my enemy, I'll sacrifice a chicken to you. I'll catch a mouse for you." They even bow to the spirits of toads and mice. The ghosts and spirits, tempted by the offer of food, are persuaded to use their spiritual, ghostly, or demonic powers to cause the victim such terrible pain that he so dies.

Ghosts and spirits occupy large trees that are several hundreds of years old. It is not that the trees themselves are spirits, as many people think. People pray to tree spirits, saying things like, "Help me win at the horse races, and I'll build you a temple." The spirit may help them win, but their winning is actually a mistake in cause and effect.

They kill living beings. People not only pray to spirits, they bribe them with fish, meat, and liquor. The spirits greedily drink the liquor, and once they are drunk, they cause a lot of trouble. With ghosts and spirits being so greedy for bribes, it is no wonder there are corrupt officials in the world.

People slaughter animals in order **to make sacrifices of blood and flesh to the** *yakṣa* **and** *rākṣasa* **ghosts.** *Yakṣas* have many names. They are known as "flying ghosts," "speedy ghosts," "life-demanding ghosts," and "money-guarding ghosts." *Rākṣasas* are powerful ghosts that eat people.

They write down the names of their enemies and make images of them. Their "enemy" refers to someone who has crossed them. They write down his name and the date and time of his birth, and they make an image of him. **And then they hex those names and images with evil mantras.** They recite deadly mantras and curse the victim, saying, "Die sooner! Die tomorrow, don't wait till the day after!" Mantras are true words that bring a response when recited with sincerity.

Once the evil ghosts and spirits accept your offerings and drink the liquor, they go about manifesting their powers and causing mischief. So don't think you're so great just because you've had some responses with the esoteric practices. You haven't opened the heavenly eye, so you don't know what's really going on! They're just a bunch of filthy ghosts and spirits that drink liquor, eat meat, and act in unruly ways.

They summon paralysis ghosts—*kumbhāṇḍa* ghosts. This type of ghost sits on sleeping people so that they cannot move or make any sound. The more nervous the victim becomes, the more the paralysis sets in. *Kumbhāṇḍa* ghosts are called "barrel-shaped ghosts" and "wintermelon ghosts," because they resemble large winter squash and earthenware jugs or barrels. These powerful ghosts may paralyze people until they die.

Some people **cast hexes.** This refers to a practice called "sticking someone with *gu* poison." If you are poisoned, you will be controlled by the person who placed it. If you don't listen to him, he can activate the poison and cause you unbearable pain.

Or command corpse-raising ghosts. This kind of black magic really exists. In the provinces of Yunnan and Guang-xi in China, people use mantras to summon corpse-raising ghosts. As soon as they recite the mantra, the corpse can stand up and walk, but only at night. The mantra doesn't work during the day, because the ghost is afraid of light.

To kill or injure their enemies. They command the corpse-raising ghost to kill the victim or to bring him under their control. They may cause the victim's stomach to be filled with worms, to the point that no doctor can cure him.

Or they may cause "stones" to grow in the victim's eyes so that he cannot see clearly. These are bizarre illnesses.

However, if the victims of such secret plots **hear the name of Medicine Master Vaiḍūrya Light Tathāgata, then all those evil things will lose their power to do harm.** The paralysis ghosts, hexes, complicated legal disputes, harmful plots, and prayers to the ghosts and spirits of mountain forests, trees, graves, and so forth will all be rendered useless. If these beings get to hear the name of Medicine Master Buddha, they will enjoy good fortune and be safe from disaster.

The evildoers will become kind to one another. The people who cast hexes or cursed people with mantras will develop a sense of compassion. **They will attain benefit, peace, and happiness and no longer cherish thoughts of malice, affliction, or enmity.** Those evil ghosts, spirits, demons, and followers of deviant cults will no longer be afflicted, nor will they be suspicious or resentful of others. **Everyone will rejoice and feel content with what they have.** The evil beings will reform and become joyful, and will not employ any more hexes, paralysis ghosts, or other demonic dharmas to harm people. They will be satisfied with what they have, and will no longer be greedy or malicious. **Instead of encroaching upon** and harming **each other, they will seek to benefit one another.** They will forgive each other, help each other out, and get along harmoniously.

[Note: Because the tapes of the Venerable Master's commentary of two sections of the Sutra are missing, two sections were re-lectured by two disciples. The following is the first re-lectured section.]

113

Sutra:

"Moreover, Mañjuśrī, there may be those among the fourfold assembly of Bhikshus, Bhikshunis, Upasakas and Upasikas, as well as other good men and women of pure faith, who accept and uphold the eight precepts either for one year or for three months, practicing and studying them. With these good roots, they may vow to be born in the Western Land of Ultimate Bliss where the Buddha of Limitless Life dwells, to hear the Proper Dharma, but their resolve may not be firm. However, if they hear the name of the World Honored One, Medicine Master Vaiḍūrya Light Tathāgata, then as the end of their lives draws near, before them will appear eight great Bodhisattvas, whose names are: Mañjuśrī Bodhisattva, The Bodhisattva Who Observes the Sounds of the World, Great Strength Bodhisattva, Inexhaustible Intention Bodhisattva, Jewelled Udumbara Flower Bodhisattva, Medicine King Bodhisattva, Medicine Superior Bodhisattva, and Maitreya Bodhisattva. Those eight great Bodhisattvas will appear in space to show them the way, and they will naturally be born by transformation in that land, amid precious flowers of a myriad colors."

Commentary:

The Buddha calls out again, "**Moreover, Mañjuśrī, there may be those among the fourfold assembly of** Buddhist disciples, namely, **Bhikshus** (fully ordained monks), **Bhikshunis** (fully ordained nuns), **Upasakas** (Buddhist laymen), **and Upasikas** (Buddhist laywomen), **as well as other good**

114

men and women of pure faith who accept and uphold the eight precepts *[the eight restrictions which include not eating at improper times]* either for one year or for three months, practicing and studying them." The three months are the first, fifth, and ninth lunar months, also known as the months of purity. It is said that during these three months, the Four Heavenly Kings come to inspect Jambudvīpa *[our "continent"]*. The merit and virtue of maintaining the rules of purity and fostering blessings during these three months is greater than in ordinary times.

If these good men and women are able to receive, uphold, and study these eight pure precepts, then, **with these good roots, they may vow to be born in the Western Land of Ultimate Bliss where the Buddha of Limitless Life dwells, to hear the Proper Dharma.** With the merit from upholding the eight precepts, they may vow to be born in the Western Land of Amitābha Buddha, where they can hear the Proper Dharma. **But their resolve may not be firm.** They may not have completely decided whether or not they really want to go.

However, if they hear the name of the World Honored One, Medicine Master Vaiḍūrya Light Tathāgata, then as the end of their lives draws near, before them will appear eight great Bodhisattvas to guide them, **whose names are: Mañjuśrī Bodhisattva, The Bodhisattva Who Observes the Sounds of the World** (Avalokiteśvara), **Great Strength** (Mahāsthāmaprāpta) **Bodhisattva, Inexhaustible Intention** (Akṣayamati) **Bodhisattva, Jewelled Udumbara Flower Bodhisattva, Medicine King** (Bhaiṣajyarāja) **Bodhisattva, Medicine Superior** (Bhaiṣajyasamudgata) **Bodhisattva, and Maitreya Bodhisattva.**

Those eight great Bodhisattvas, by means of their spiritual powers, **will appear in space** before these people at their time of death **to show them the way,** leading them to rebirth in the Eastern Pure Land. **And they will naturally be born by transformation in that land, amid precious flowers of a myriad colors.** That Pure Land has a profusion of colorful flowers: green colored of green light, yellow colored of yellow light, red colored of red light, and white colored of white light. The eight great Bodhisattvas will guide cultivators to the Eastern Vaiḍūrya Land, where they will be born purely and by transformation, without having to pass through a mother's womb.

Sutra:

"Or they may be born in the heavens due to this cause. Although reborn in the heavens, their original good roots will not be exhausted, and so they will not fall into the evil destinies again. When their life in the heavens ends, they will be born among people again. They may be wheel-turning kings, reigning over the four continents with awesome virtue and ease, bringing uncountable hundreds of thousands of living beings to abide in the practice of the ten good deeds. Or they may be born as *kṣatriyas*, Brahmans, laymen, or sons of honorable families. They will be wealthy, with storehouses filled to overflowing. Handsome in appearance, they will be surrounded by a great retinue of relatives. They will be intelligent and wise, courageous and valiant, like great and awesome knights. If a woman hears the name of the World Honored One, Medicine Master Vaiḍūrya Light Tathāgata, and sincerely cherishes it, in the future she will never again be born as a female."

Commentary:

Or they may be born in the heavens due to this cause. By virtue of Medicine Master Buddha's vows, cultivators who vow to be reborn in a pure land can do so, and those who have not made vows to go to a pure land can still enjoy the blessings of birth in the heavens. **Although reborn in the heavens, their original good roots will not be exhausted, and so they will not fall into the evil destinies again.** Ordinarily, those born in the heavens enjoy blessings "with outflows," and when those blessings end, they fall into the lower realms again. When beings are born in the heavens through hearing the name of Medicine Master Buddha, however, their original good roots will not come to an end, and they will not fall into the paths of the hells, hungry ghosts, and animals.

When their life in the heavens ends, when their heavenly blessings run out, **they will be born among people again. They may be wheel-turning kings, reigning over the four continents.** There are four kinds of wheel-turning sage kings:

1. Gold wheel-turning kings reign over the four great continents: Pūrvavideha in the East, Jambudvīpa in the South, Aparagodāniya in the West, and Uttarakuru in the North.
2. Silver wheel-turning kings rule the three continents in the south, west, and east.
3. Copper wheel-turning kings rule the two continents in the south and west.

4. Iron wheel-turning kings, the lowest kind, rule over the one continent in the south.

As wheel-turning sage kings, they are endowed **with awesome virtue and ease, bringing uncountable hundreds of thousands of living beings to abide in the practice of the ten good deeds.** They influence countless beings to practice the ten good deeds.

The three deeds involving the karma of the body are:

1. Not killing, which means not taking the life of any creature;
2. Not stealing, which means not taking what has not been given to one;
3. Not engaging in sexual misconduct, which means not having improper sexual relations with any man or woman.

The four deeds involving the karma of the mouth are:

4. Not lying, which means always speaking truthfully;
5. Not speaking harshly, which means not berating or speaking rudely to others;
6. Not speaking duplicitously, which means not speaking of others' faults or sowing seeds of dissension;
7. Not speaking frivolously, which means avoiding obscenities, off-color jokes, and idle chatter.

The three deeds involving the karma of the mind are:

8. Not being greedy,
9. Not being hateful,
10. Not being deluded.

The opposites of these ten good deeds are the ten evil deeds.

Cultivators may become wheel-turning sage kings, **or they may be born as** *kṣatriyas*, **Brahmans, laymen, or sons of honorable families.** They may be born into a royal family, into a family of Brahmans (those who cultivate purity), into a family of orthodox Buddhists, or into an old and respectable family whose members are well-educated.

They will be wealthy, with storehouses of gold, silver, and valuables **filled to overflowing.** They enjoy all the material comforts, such as an inexhaustible supply of food and provisions, and clothes of the finest quality. **Handsome in appearance, they will be surrounded by a great retinue of relatives.** Everyone is delighted to see them. All their relatives get along well and help each other. **They will be intelligent and wise.** They are learned in many subjects and understand many principles. They have great wisdom, and are talented in both mental and physical disciplines. They are **courageous and valiant, like great and awesome knights.** They are strong and heroic. Up to this point, the passage has been talking about being born in the human realm, not only with a healthy and perfect body, but as a man.

If a woman hears the name of the World Honored One, Medicine Master Vaiḍūrya Light Tathāgata, and sincerely cherishes it, in the future she will obtain an inconceivable response and **never again be born as a female.** In life after life, she will not have to undergo the suffering of being female. That is, in effect, to turn from being female into being male.

Sutra:

"**Moreover, Mañjuśrī, when Medicine Master Vaiḍūrya Light Tathāgata attained Bodhi, by the power of**

119

his past vows he contemplated all the sentient beings who were undergoing various kinds of sicknesses and sufferings. Some suffered from diseases such as emaciation, atrophy, severe thirst, or yellow fever; others were harmed by paralysis ghosts or by poisonous hexes; some died naturally when young, while others experienced untimely deaths. He wished to dispel all their sicknesses and sufferings, and to fulfill their wishes."

Commentary:

Moreover, Mañjuśrī, when Medicine Master Vaiḍūrya Light Tathāgata attained Bodhi, by the power of his past vows he contemplated all the sentient beings who were undergoing various kinds of sicknesses and sufferings. In past lives, Medicine Master Buddha made great vows to become a great king of physicians so that he would be able to cure living beings' 84,000 sicknesses (which represent an infinite number of sicknesses). Imbalance of the four elements (earth, water, fire and air) in our bodies, possession by ghosts or spirits, and karma from past lives are some of the reasons that we become ill.

Some suffered from diseases such as emaciation, atrophy, severe thirst, or yellow fever. Emaciation causes a person to waste away until he is mere skin and bones. Atrophy refers to a kind of disease that cripples a person so that he cannot straighten his hands or feet. Day by day, his limbs wither and shrink. There is also a disease of thirst, called *ganxiao*, in which the person feels parched. People with yellow fever have a jaundiced appearance. These and other diseases, such as typhoid fever and plagues, are caused by an imbalance of the four elements.

Others were harmed by paralysis ghosts or by poisonous hexes. Paralysis ghosts attack people in their sleep, pressing down on them so that they cannot move or make a sound. Sicknesses caused by poisonous hexes occur in areas where witchcraft is prevalent. In China's Yunnan province and in some parts of Southeast Asia, there are people who raise poisonous insects, such as centipedes, spiders, and scorpions, and place them in a vessel, which is then sealed with an incantation. The insects devour each other until only one is left. The last remaining insect contains all the poison of the others and is "the king of poison." Then spells and incantations are used to direct that insect, by then a monstrosity, to attack victims and cause them to become sick or die.

Some died naturally when young, due to their heavy karma from past lives, while others experienced untimely deaths, dying in various accidents such as plane crashes, train derailments, shipwrecks, car collisions, floods, fires, earthquakes, and hurricanes. Most people are totally unprepared to lose their lives under such circumstances. Medicine Master Buddha was extremely clear about such causes and effects, and he wished to dispel all their sicknesses and sufferings, and to fulfill their wishes.

Sutra:

> At that time, the World Honored One entered a samādhi called "extinguishing the suffering and distress of all beings." After he entered this samādhi, a great light came forth from his flesh-cowl. From amid that light he proclaimed this magnificent *dhāraṇī*:

121

Na mo bo qie fa di. Bi sha she. Ju lu bi liu li. Bo la
po. He la she ye. Da tuo jie duo ye. E la he di. San miao
san pu tuo ye. Da zhi tuo nan. Bi sha shi. Bi sha shi. Bi
sha she. San mo jie di. Suo he.

After he had spoken that mantra from amid the
light, the earth trembled and emitted great light. All
beings' sicknesses and sufferings were cast off, and
they felt peaceful and happy.

Commentary:

At that time, the World Honored One, Medicine Master
Vaiḍūrya Light Tathāgata, **entered a samadhi called "extinguishing the suffering and distress of all beings." After
he entered this samādhi, a great light came forth from his
flesh-cowl.** *Samādhi* is Sanskrit and means proper concen-
tration and proper reception. From the invisible appearance on the crown of Medicine Master Buddha's head, from
his flesh-cowl, he emitted a boundless light.

*[Note: This is the end of the first section
that was re-lectured by a disciple.]*

From amid that light he proclaimed this magnificent
dhāraṇī. Wishing to save and protect all living beings and
to relieve them of sickness and suffering, he spoke the mantra.

If you recite this very short mantra faithfully and single-
mindedly, you will find that it has infinitely many wonderful functions. A doctor can use this mantra to enable his
patients to have a speedy recovery. With the mantra's help,
he can become an extremely good doctor. Everyone, whether
you are a doctor or not, should recite this mantra. If you
recite it on behalf of sick people, they will soon get well.

The mantra consists of transliterated sounds, which cannot be explained. You are not supposed to understand what the mantra means. It is wonderful precisely because it is not understood. Since you can't think about what it means, you'll be able to recite single-mindedly and obtain a response. The mantra goes: *Na mo bo qie fa di. Bi sha she. Ju lu bi liu li. Bo la po. He la she ye. Da tuo jie duo ye. E la he di. San miao san pu tuo ye. Da zhi tuo nan. Bi sha shi. Bi sha shi. Bi sha she. San mo jie di. Suo he.*

If you recite this mantra constantly, there will be an inconceivable response. **After he had spoken that mantra from amid the light, the earth trembled and emitted great light.** After Medicine Master Buddha had spoken the True Words for Anointing the Crown, the earth shook in six ways: quaking, roaring, striking, moving, surging, and rising. **All beings' sicknesses and sufferings were cast off, and they felt peaceful and happy.**

Sutra:

> "Mañjuśrī, if you see a man (or a woman) who is ill, you should single-mindedly and frequently clean and bathe him and rinse his mouth. Provide him with food, medicine, or water that is free of insects, over any of which the *dhāraṇī* has been recited 108 times. After the sick person has taken it, all his sicknesses and sufferings will be gone. If this person has a wish, he should recite this mantra with utmost sincerity. Then he will obtain whatever he wished for, and his life will be prolonged and free from illness. At the end of his life, he will be reborn in that Buddha's land. He will become irreversible and will ultimately

attain Bodhi. Therefore, Mañjuśrī, if there are men
and women who, with utmost sincerity, diligently
worship and make offerings to Medicine Master
Vaiḍūrya Light Tathāgata, they should always recite
this mantra and never forget it."

Commentary:

"Mañjuśrī, if you see a man (or a woman) who is ill, you
should single-mindedly and frequently clean and bathe
him or her and rinse his or her mouth. Then the person's
body will be clean and his mind will have pure thoughts.
Provide him or her with food, medicine, or water that is
free of insects, over any of which the *dhāraṇī* has been
recited 108 times. Take the sick person's food, medicine, or
water that has no insects in it, and recite the True Words for
Anointing the Crown over it 108 times. Then give it to the
sick person. After the sick person has taken it, all his
sicknesses and sufferings will be gone.

If this person has a wish, he should recite this mantra
108 times with utmost sincerity. Then he will obtain
whatever he wished for, and his life will be prolonged
and free from illness. Even if he is supposed to die, he will
not die. That's how wonderful it is!

And at the end of his life, he will be reborn in that
Buddha's land. When it is really time for his life to end, he
will be reborn in Medicine Master Buddha's Pure Land. He
will become irreversible and will ultimately attain Bodhi.
He will advance steadily, never retreating, until he accom-
plishes the Unsurpassed, Proper and Equal, Right Enlightenment.

Therefore, Mañjuśrī, if there are men and women

who, with utmost sincerity, diligently worship and make offerings to Medicine Master Vaiḍūrya Light Tathāgata, if they are single-minded and very attentive and respectful in doing this, **they should always recite this mantra and never forget it.** They should constantly recite the True Words for Anointing the Crown and never let them slip from their memory.

Sutra:

"Moreover, Mañjuśrī, men or women of pure faith, who have heard all the names of Medicine Master Vaiḍūrya Light Tathāgata, One of Proper and Equal Enlightenment, should recite and uphold them. In the early morning, after brushing their teeth and bathing, they should make offerings of fragrant flowers, incense, perfumed balms, and various kinds of music before an image of that Buddha. They should personally write out this Sutra or ask others to do so, and they should single-mindedly and constantly recite it. If they listen to explanations of its meaning from a Dharma Master, they should make offerings to him of all necessities, so that he is without the slightest want. In this way, they will receive the mindful protection of the Buddhas. All of their wishes will be fulfilled, and they will ultimately attain Bodhi."

Commentary:

"Moreover, Mañjuśrī, men or women of pure faith, who have heard all the names of Medicine Master Vaiḍūrya Light Tathāgata, One of Proper and Equal Enlightenment, should recite and uphold them. The ten titles of Medicine

Master Buddha are: Tathāgata, One Worthy of Offerings, One of Proper and Universal Knowledge, One Whose Understanding and Practice Are Complete, Well Gone One Who Understands the World, Supreme Lord, Regulating Hero, Teacher of Gods and Humans, Buddha, and World Honored One. After hearing all these names, they should be able to recite them constantly.

In the early morning when they get up, **after brushing their teeth** by chewing on a willow twig [a custom in the Buddha's time], rinsing their mouth, **and bathing** so that they are clean and pure, **they should make offerings of fragrant flowers, incense, perfumed balms, and various kinds of music before an image of that Buddha** in order to worship Medicine Master Buddha or the *Sutra of the Merit and Virtue of the Past Vows of Medicine Master Vaiḍūrya Light Tathāgata.* **They should personally write out this Sutra or ask others to do so, and they should single-mindedly and constantly recite it.** They may also single-mindedly recite Medicine Master Buddha's name.

If they listen to explanations of its meaning from a Dharma Master, they should make offerings to him of all necessities, so that he is without the slightest want. If there is a Dharma Master who explains, writes out, receives and upholds, or recites the Sutra, the laypeople should reverently provide him with the Four Kinds of Offerings— food (pure vegetarian meals), clothing, bedding, and medicines. They should make sure the Dharma Master does not lack these basic necessities.

In this way they will receive the mindful protection of the Buddhas. If one supports a Dharma Master who writes out, receives, upholds, or recites the *Medicine Master Sutra,* the Buddhas of the ten directions will mindfully protect one. **All of their wishes will be fulfilled, and they will ultimately attain Bodhi.**

Disciples of the Buddha should treat the study of the Dharma as more important than anything—more important than their studies at school, more important than their jobs and careers. One of my disciples told of how she became a vegetarian and started coming to Sutra lectures after the "Three Steps One Bow" monks came and lectured on the Sutras. This is very rare. Simply by cherishing the Sutra lectures, you are being a good disciple of the Buddha. We should be very sincere in listening to the lectures.

Sutra:

> At that time, the Pure Youth Mañjuśrī said to the Buddha, "World Honored One, I vow that in the Dharma Image Age, using various expedient means, I shall enable good men and women of pure faith to hear the name of the World Honored One, Medicine Master Vaiḍūrya Light Tathāgata. Even during their sleep, I will awaken them with this Buddha's name."

Commentary:

At that time, the Pure Youth Mañjuśrī, the Dharma Prince, **said to the Buddha, "World Honored One,** who is honored both in and beyond the world, **I vow that in the Dharma ImageAge** of the future, **using various expedient means,** I shall teach the Dharma to living beings in accord with their dispositions. I will wisely select expedient methods to teach them.

"**I shall enable good men and women of pure faith to**

hear the name of the World Honored One, Medicine Master Vaiḍūrya Light Tathāgata. Even during their sleep, I will awaken them with this Buddha's name. If the conditions ripen when they are asleep, I will enable them to hear the name of that Buddha in their dreams, so that they will wake up and cultivate the Buddhadharma."

What is the Dharma Image Age? The Buddhadharma goes through three phases called the Proper Dharma Age, the Dharma Image Age, and the Dharma Ending Age. During the Proper Dharma Age, which starts when the Buddha is dwelling in the world and lasts for 500 or 1,000 years, many people like to meditate and develop samādhi. During this age, people emphasize the inner skill of sages. During the Dharma Image Age which follows, people become attached to appearances. They are skilled at constructing temples and monasteries, which can be considered the outward-looking skill of kings. Although they build many temples to support Buddhism, they are concerned only with appearances. There are many cultivators in the Proper Dharma Age, but few in the Dharma Image Age. The Dharma Image Age can be considered to last for 1,000 years, although some say it is 500 years.

We live in the Dharma Ending Age, which is very distant from the Buddha's time. In the Dharma Ending Age, people are skilled not in meditation or building temples, but in fighting. People fight with people, families fight with families, countries fight with countries, and planets fight with planets. People are constantly fighting and terrorizing each others. This is truly an age of terror. Perhaps because we did not do any good deeds, we have been born in the Dharma Ending Age, when Buddhism is nearing its demise. We will consider the Dharma Ending Age to be 10,000 years long, although some people say it will last for only 1,000 years.

It has been more than three thousand years since the Buddha's time. The Proper Dharma Age and the Dharma Image Age each lasted for a thousand years, and now we are one thousand years into the Dharma Ending Age. Although we were not lucky enough to see the supreme conditions that existed in the Buddha's time, we should make vows to propagate the Proper Dharma in the present time and to turn the Dharma-Ending Age into the Proper Dharma Age. If we all make this vow, the Dharma will not become extinct. Buddhism has just come to the West, and we must staunchly support and propagate the Proper Dharma; we must take the Proper Dharma as our standard in all we do; the Proper Dharma is our goal and purpose. We should all make a great Bodhi resolve and protect the Treasury of the Proper Dharma Eye.

Sutra:

> "World Honored One, there may be those who accept and uphold this Sutra, read and recite it, explain its meanings for others, write it out themselves, or tell others to write it out. They may revere it by making offerings of various flowers, paste incense, powdered incense, stick incense, flower garlands, necklaces, banners, canopies, and music. They may make bags of five-colored thread in which to keep the Sutra. They may sweep clean a place and arrange a high altar on which to place this Sutra. At that time, the Four

Heavenly Kings with their retinues and other innumerable hundreds of thousands of gods will come
to that place to worship and protect it.

"World Honored One, it should be known that if,
in the places where this precious Sutra circulates,
people can accept and uphold it, then due to the merit
and virtue of the past vows of that World Honored
One, Medicine Master Vaiḍūrya Light Tathāgata,
because they have heard his name, none of those
people will meet with untimely death. In addition,
none of them will be robbed of his vital energy by evil
ghosts and spirits. Those people whose vital energies
have already been robbed will have their health
restored, and they will be happy and at peace in body
and mind."

Commentary:

Mañjuśrī Bodhisattva calls out again, **"World Honored
One,** you who are honored both in the world and beyond
it, in the Dharma Image Age as well as the Dharma Ending
Age, **there may be those who accept and uphold this
Sutra, read** it from the book **and recite it** from memory,
explain its meanings for others." Based upon your own
wisdom and understanding of the Sutra, you may expound
it for others, illustrating its wonderful principles and its
great importance through the use of analogies.

Write it out themselves or tell others to write it out.
You may write out the Sutra on paper with brush and ink,
or you may tell others to write it out. **They may revere it by**
bowing to it, or by setting the Sutra on the altar and **making
offerings of various flowers, paste incense, powdered**

incense, stick incense, flower garlands, necklaces, banners, canopies, and music. One may play various kinds of music in praise to the Buddha as an offering to this Sutra.

They may make bags of five-colored thread in which to keep the Sutra. They may sweep clean a place in their house and arrange a high altar on which to place this Sutra. To show their respect, they keep the Sutra in a high place.

At that time, the Four Heavenly Kings with their retinues and other innumerable hundreds of thousands of gods will come to that place where offerings are made to the Sutra, to worship and protect it.

World Honored One, it should be known that if, in the places where this precious Sutra circulates, people can accept and uphold it, then due to the merit and virtue of the past vows of that World Honored One, Medicine Master Vaiḍūrya Light Tathāgata, and because they have heard his name, none of those people will meet with untimely death. Accidental deaths will not occur in any place where this Sutra is found.

In addition, none of them will be robbed of his vital energy by evil ghosts and spirits. Those people whose vital energies have already been robbed will be restored to health, and they will be happy and at peace in body and mind. If people's essence and energy have been depleted by evil ghosts and spirits, they will be restored to health. They will be free from afflictions, disasters, and misfortunes. If you think your home is haunted by ghosts, take home a copy of the *Sutra of the Merit and Virtue of the Past Vows of Medicine Master Vaiḍūrya Light Tathāgata* and make offerings to it. This is the best way to chase away evil influences and bring peace to a household.

Sutra:

The Buddha told Mañjuśrī, "So it is, so it is! It is exactly as you say. Mañjuśrī, if there are good men and women of pure faith who wish to make offerings to that World Honored One, Medicine Master Vaiḍūrya Light Tathāgata, they should first make an image of that Buddha and arrange a pure and clean dais on which to place the image. Then they should strew all kinds of flowers, burn various incenses, and adorn the place with a variety of banners and streamers. For seven days and seven nights they should hold the eight precepts and eat pure food. Having bathed until clean and fragrant, they should put on clean clothes. Their minds should be undefiled, without thoughts of anger and malice. Toward all sentient beings, they should cherish thoughts of benevolence, peace, kindness, compassion, joy, giving, and equanimity.

"Playing musical instruments and singing praises, they should circumambulate to the right of the Buddha's image. Moreover, they should recall the merit and virtue of that Tathāgata's past vows. They should read and recite this Sutra, ponder its meaning, and lecture on and explain it. Then they will obtain whatever they seek: Those who seek long life will attain longevity; those who seek wealth will gain wealth; those who seek an official position will obtain it; and those who seek a son or a daughter will have one."

Commentary:

The Buddha told Mañjuśrī Bodhisattva, "So it is, so it is!

You're right! It is exactly as you say. Mañjuśrī, if there are good men and women of pure faith who wish to make offerings to that World Honored One, Medicine Master Vaiḍūrya Light Tathāgata, they should first make an image of that Buddha and arrange a pure and spotlessly clean dais on which to place the image so that offerings can be made to it. Then they should strew all kinds of flowers, burn various incenses, and adorn the place with a variety of banners and streamers."

When we make offerings to Buddhas and Bodhisattvas, we should not think that they are as greedy as we are, always hoping someone will invite them for tea or a vegetarian meal. We offer fine incense, fresh flowers, and so forth to show our sincerity, but that doesn't mean the Buddhas and Bodhisattvas enjoy these things. They aren't delighted if we burn incense for them, and they don't get upset if we don't. They don't need any of the worldly things that people offer to them. We make such offerings only because we have no other way of showing our sincerity.

When we make offerings, we should not be like those superstitious people who light big handfuls of joss sticks in front of the Buddha. When they burn so much incense, the Buddha, who had been peacefully shining his protective light on living beings, disappears in a cloud of smoke and can't even open his eyes! That causes him to stop shining his light and protecting people. Of course this is just my foolish conjecture about the Buddha's state, but my point is, there's no need to offer great big handfuls of incense to the Buddha. It would be like covering a hundred-foot-long table with food and expecting one person to eat it all.

We should light no more than three sticks of incense as

an offering to the Buddha, with perhaps one more stick for the Dharma-protecting spirits, making four sticks in all. Usually, one stick of incense is enough. If you are sincere, the Bodhisattvas will protect you even if you don't offer incense. The Buddhas will be happy as long as you are mindful of the Triple Jewel and you recite the Sutras. You don't need to light incense to make them happy.

Ordinary people dislike criticism and are fond of praise, but Buddhas are not so petty. Our common minds cannot fathom the wisdom of sages. Don't think Buddhas are as greedy as people. Don't be like the superstitious folk who worship in the temples, thinking, "The more money we give and the more incense we burn, the better." They are very sure that their attitude is correct, but they can't explain why. Now wouldn't you say that they are muddled? Buddhists should listen to truth and wisdom and not be superstitious.

For seven days and seven nights, they should hold the eight precepts and eat pure food that does not contain meat or pungent plants *[onions, garlic, leeks, shallots, and chives].* **Having bathed until clean and fragrant, they should put on clean clothes.** They should wash the sweat and grime off their bodies and bathe in fragrant water so that they smell nice, and then put on clean, but not necessarily fancy, clothes. Their clothes can be very coarse, but as long as they are clean, they are being respectful toward the Buddhas.

Their minds should be undefiled, without thoughts of anger and malice. Purify your mind. Cast out the garbage and defilements. Don't harbor thoughts of anger and harm.

Toward all sentient beings, they should cherish

thoughts of benevolence, peace, kindness, compassion, joy, giving, and equanimity. They should wish peace and well-being upon all beings. **Playing musical instruments and singing praises, they should circumambulate to the right of the Buddha's image.**

Moreover, they should recall and recite the Sutra of the merit and virtue of that Tathāgata's past vows. They should read and recite this Sutra, ponder its meaning, and lecture on and explain it. Then they will obtain whatever they seek. Those who seek long life will attain longevity; those who seek wealth will gain wealth; those who seek an official position will obtain it; and those who seek a son or a daughter will have one. How great are the merits of this *Sutra of the Merit and Virtue of the Past Vows of Medicine Master Vaiḍūrya Light Tathāgata*! As long as you are sincere, your prayers will be answered.

Sutra:

"Moreover, if a person who suddenly has nightmares, sees ill omens, notices strange birds flocking together, or perceives many uncanny events in his dwelling can worship and make offerings of many fine things to that World Honored One, Medicine Master Vaiḍūrya Light Tathāgata, then the nightmares, ill omens, and inauspicious things will disappear and will no longer trouble him.

"When a person is endangered by water, fire, knives, or poison; or finds himself on a steep cliff or in a dangerous place; or faces fierce elephants, lions, tigers, wolves, bears, poisonous snakes, scorpions, centipedes, millipedes, mosquitoes, gnats, or other

> frightful things, if he can single-mindedly recollect, worship, and make offerings to that Buddha, he will be liberated from all those frightful things. When other countries invade or when there are thieves or riots, if a person can recollect and worship that Tathāgata, then he will be free of all of these as well."

Commentary:

Moreover, if a person who suddenly has nightmares, who dreams that he himself or someone else dies, or is in a car accident, or jumps into the sea—all kinds of unlucky dreams, or **sees ill omens...** Maybe he sees a hideous *rākṣasa* ghost, or a monster with fangs and a huge mouth, or the Thunder God preparing to strike people with his thunderbolt. He may dream of earthquakes, avalanches, tidal waves, or other bad omens.

Or it may be that he **notices** a lot of **strange birds flocking together** over his house, unusual birds such as horned owls, eared owls, and crows. **Or he perceives many uncanny events in his dwelling,** such as ghosts in the daytime, or demons in the night, or a broomstick walking around by itself, or a soup ladle flying through the house.

If he or others in such a household **can worship and make offerings of many fine things,** the most precious and valuable things, **to that World Honored One, Medicine Master Vaiḍūrya Light Tathāgata, then the nightmares, ill omens, and inauspicious events will disappear and will no longer trouble him.** All his bad dreams—perhaps dreams about snakes, tigers, wolves, leopards, or other beasts—and all the unlucky things will be gone before he knows it. Therefore, if you think your home is haunted, worship and make offerings to Medicine Master Buddha, and your problems will disappear and you will obtain good luck.

When a person is endangered by being drowned in deep water, burned by fire, harmed by knives or poison; or finds himself on a steep cliff or in a dangerous place; or faces fierce elephants—such as an intoxicated elephant that is ready to kill anyone it sees, man-eating lions, tigers, wolves, bears, poisonous snakes, scorpions, poisonous centipedes, millipedes, which burrow into people's brains and suck them dry, mosquitoes, gnats, or other harmful creatures or frightful things; if he can single-mindedly recollect Medicine Master Vaiḍūrya Light Tathāgata, worship, and make offerings to that Buddha, he will be liberated from all those frightful things. He will no longer have anything to fear.

When other countries invade or when there are thieves or riots within the country, if a person can recollect and worship that Tathāgata in thought after thought, then he will be free of all of these disasters as well. All misfortunes will turn into good luck.

Sutra:

"Moreover, Mañjuśrī, there may be good men and women of pure faith who, all their lives, do not worship other gods, but single-mindedly take refuge with the Buddha, the Dharma, and the Saṅgha. They accept and uphold precepts, such as the five precepts, the ten precepts, the four hundred precepts of a Bodhisattva, the two hundred and fifty precepts of a Bhikshu, or the five hundred precepts of a Bhikshuni.

Perhaps they have violated some of the precepts they received and are afraid of falling into the evil destinies. If they concentrate on reciting that Buddha's name and worship and make offerings to him, they definitely will not be reborn in the three evil destinies.

"If there is a woman about to give birth who suffers great pain, if she sincerely recites his name and worships, praises, venerates, and makes offerings to that Tathāgata, all her sufferings will be dispelled. The newborn child will be sound and healthy, and will have upright features. Seeing him will make people happy. He will be keen and intelligent, peaceful and secure, and with few ailments, and no evil spirit will come to rob him of his vitality."

Commentary:

"**Moreover,**" says Sākyamuni Buddha, "Mañjuśrī, let me tell you more. **There may be good men and women of pure faith,** virtuous men and women **who, all their lives, do not worship other gods.** They do not worship heavenly or earthly deities, ghosts, spirits, or gods of non-Buddhist religions, **but single-mindedly** and with utmost sincerity **take refuge with the Buddha, the Dharma, and the Saṅgha.**

They receive and strictly **uphold** the Buddha's **precepts, such as the five precepts,** which prohibit killing, stealing, sexual misconduct, lying, and taking intoxicants, **the ten precepts** of a Shramanera (novice), **the four hundred precepts of a Bodhisattva, the two hundred and fifty precepts of a Bhikshu, or the five hundred precepts of a Bhikshuni.**

Perhaps they have violated, whether deliberately and not, some of the precepts they received and are afraid of falling into the evil destinies. If they concentrate on reciting that Buddha's name, sincerely and single-mindedly reciting, "Homage to Medicine Master Buddha Who Quells Disasters and Lengthens Life," and worship and make offerings to him wholeheartedly, they definitely will not be reborn in the three evil destinies.

If there is a woman about to give birth who suffers unbearably great pain, if she sincerely recites his name and worships, praises, venerates, and makes offerings to that Tathāgata, all her sufferings will be dispelled. The newborn child will be sound and healthy. The baby's physical faculties will be complete and perfect. He will not be missing an eye, ear, nose, or mouth.

He will have upright features. Seeing him will make people happy. Everyone will like to see this child. He will be keen and intelligent, peaceful and secure, and with few ailments, and no evil spirit will come to rob him of his vitality. He will be extremely bright and will seldom be ill. His essence will not be absorbed by goblins, demons, ghosts, or other evil spirits, because the awesome spiritual power of Medicine Master Buddha will keep such beings away from him.

Today I want to tell you which Bodhisattva the people of Los Angeles have affinities with. The climate of Los Angeles is similar to that of Jiuhua ("Nine Flowers") Mountain in China *[the Bodhimaṇḍa of Earth Store Bodhisattva]*. The causes and conditions of these two places are very similar. Therefore, all of you in Los Angeles have great affinities with Earth Store Bodhisattva. Earth Store

Bodhisattva is the host of Gold Wheel Monastery and Guanyin Bodhisattva is its Dharma protector. At the City of Ten Thousand Buddhas, Guanshiyin Bodhisattva is the host and Earth Store Bodhisattva acts as Dharma protector. The City is Guanyin's *bodhimaṇḍa*, since its climate is similar to that of Mount Putuo *[Guanyin Bodhisattva's bodhimaṇḍa in China]*. Universal Worthy Bodhisattva's *bodhimaṇḍa* is in Seattle (which is similar to Mount Emei, Universal Worthy's *bodhimaṇḍa* in China), and Mañjuśrī Bodhisattva's *bodhimaṇḍa* is in Vancouver (which is comparable to Wutai Mountain in China). Mañjuśrī likes the cold, so I have chosen Vancouver to be the site of his *bodhimaṇḍa*. This Bodhisattva often appears there and emits light. In Seattle, Universal Worthy Bodhisattva is the host and Mañjuśrī Bodhisattva is the Dharma protector. In Vancouver, Mañjuśrī Bodhisattva is the host, and Universal Worthy Bodhisattva is the Dharma protector.

Instead of travelling all the way to China, you can worship Guanyin Bodhisattva at the City of Ten Thousand Buddhas. Worshipping Earth Store Bodhisattva at Gold Wheel Monastery is just like going to Jiuhua Mountain to worship him. And at our temple in Vancouver, you can pay homage to Mañjuśrī Bodhisattva just as if you were at Wutai Mountain in China. I have invited the four great Bodhisattvas to come to these four temples, so you can pay homage to them without travelling the great distance to China.

Although you may not see them, I feel that the four great Bodhisattvas are now at these four *bodhimaṇḍas*. Whether you believe this or not is up to you.

*[Note: The next section of the Sutra
was lectured by a disciple.]*

Sutra:

At that time the World Honored One said to Ananda,
"The merit and virtue of the World Honored One,
Medicine Master Vaiḍūrya Light Tathāgata, which I
have just extolled, is the extremely profound practice
of all Buddhas. It is difficult to fathom and to comprehend. Do you believe it or not?"

Commentary:

Disciples of the Buddha must have true faith and sincere
vows before they can obtain actual benefit. Thus, the
Flower Adornment Sutra says, "Faith is the source of the
Way and the mother of merit and virtue. It nurtures all
good roots." Without faith, you cannot foster good roots or
merit and virtue.

At that time, the World Honored One said to Ananda,
"All the inconceivable **merit and virtue of the World**
Honored One, Medicine Master Vaiḍūrya Light Tathā-
gata, which I have just extolled, is the extremely profound
practice of all Buddhas. This is the state of the most
profound and wondrous practice of all Buddhas. **It is**
difficult to fathom and to comprehend. Only Buddhas and
those who have gone through the experience can understand it. Ordinary people cannot conceive of it. **Do you**
believe it or not? Now, Ananda, do you truly believe
everything I have told you? Are you free of doubts?"

Sutra:

Ananda said, "Greatly virtuous World Honored One,

I have absolutely no doubts regarding the Sutras spoken by the Tathāgata. Why? Because all Buddhas' karmas of body, speech, and mind are pure. World Honored One, the sun and moon could fall, Wonderfully High, the king of mountains, could be toppled or shaken, but the words of the Buddhas never change."

Commentary:

Ananda said in reply, "Greatly virtuous World Honored One, I have absolutely no doubts regarding the Sutras spoken by the Tathāgata. The Sutras ('tallying texts') tally with the principles of all Buddhas above and with the potentials of all living beings below. I have not the slightest doubt regarding them. Why? Because all Buddhas' karmas of body, speech and mind are completely pure, without even a speck of defilement or falseness.

"World Honored One, between heaven and earth, the sun and moon could fall, Wonderfully High, which is just Mount Sumeru, the king of mountains, could be toppled or shaken, and everything else could change, but the words of the Buddhas never change. The words of every Buddha are absolutely true and cannot be altered."

Sutra:

"World Honored One, there are sentient beings deficient in faith who hear about the extremely profound practices of all Buddhas and think to themselves, 'How could one obtain such supreme merit and benefit merely by reciting the name of a single Buddha, Medicine Master Vaiḍūrya Light Tathāgata?' Due to this lack of faith, they give rise to slander. During the long night, they lose great benefit and joy and fall into the evil destinies, where they wander ceaselessly."

Commentary:

"World Honored One, there are sentient beings deficient in faith, who are particularly skeptical and lack the foundations of faith, who hear about the extremely profound practices of all Buddhas and think to themselves... When they hear about the conduct of all Buddhas, about the unfathomably deep wisdom and the blessings, virtue, and wonderful functioning of the spiritual penetrations of all Buddhas, they immediately become doubtful. They think, 'How could one obtain such immeasurable supreme merit and benefit merely by reciting the name of a single Buddha, Medicine Master Vaiḍūrya Light Tathāgata?' Due to this lack of faith, they give rise to slander. Their doubts lead them to think, "The Buddha cheats people. Everything he says is a lie." Their reckless slander causes people to lose faith in the Triple Jewel.

During the long night, they lose great benefit and joy and fall into the evil destinies, where they wander ceaselessly. During the endless night, which is an analogy for the endless rounds of birth and death, they forsake all benefits and happiness and suffer in the hells, the hungry ghost realm, and the animal realm.

Sutra:

The Buddha told Ananda, "If these sentient beings hear the name of the World Honored One, Medicine Master Vaiḍūrya Light Tathāgata, and sincerely accept and uphold it without any doubts, they cannot possibly fall into the evil destinies.

"Ananda, this is the extremely profound practice of all Buddhas which is difficult to believe and to understand! You should know that your ability to accept this comes from the awesome power of the Tathāgata. Ananda, all Hearers, Solitarily Enlightened Ones, and the Bodhisattvas who have not yet ascended to the Grounds are incapable of believing and understanding this Dharma as it really is. Only the Bodhisattvas who are destined in one life to attain Buddhahood are capable of understanding.

"Ananda, it is difficult to obtain a human body. It is also difficult to have faith in and to revere the Triple Jewel. It is even more difficult to be able to hear the name of the World Honored One, Medicine Master Vaiḍūrya Light Tathāgata. Ananda, Medicine Master Vaiḍūrya Light Tathāgata possesses boundless Bodhisattva practices, limitless skillful expedients, and immeasurably vast, great vows. If I were to speak extensively of those for an eon or more, the eon would soon end, but that Buddha's practices, vows, and skillful expedients have no end!"

Commentary:

The Buddha further told Ananda, "If these living beings, the ones mentioned above, are able to **hear the name of the World Honored One, Medicine Master Vaiḍūrya Light Tathāgata, and sincerely** and single-mindedly **accept and uphold it without any doubts, they cannot possibly fall into the evil destinies.** There would be absolutely no chance that such people would fall into the three evil destinies. **Ananda, this is the extremely profound practice of all Buddhas which is difficult to believe and to understand!** The Buddhas' deeds are based on extremely profound wisdom, which ordinary people find hard to believe and understand.

You should know that your ability to believe and **accept this comes** not from your own power, but **from the awesome power of the Tathāgata.** It is through the aid of the Buddha's awesome spiritual power that you can have such absolute faith. Why do I say this?

Ananda, all Hearers, Solitarily Enlightened Ones, and the Bodhisattvas who have not yet ascended to the Grounds are incapable of believing and understanding this Dharma as it really is. Not to mention ordinary people, even those who have attained to the first, second, third, or fourth fruitions of Arhatship, Pratyekabuddhas, and Bodhisattvas who have not yet entered the First Ground are unable to bring forth such genuine faith and understanding. **Only the Bodhisattvas who are destined in one life to attain Buddhahood, are capable of understanding.** Only those who have reached the position of Equal Enlightenment, Bodhisattvas who will attain Buddhahood in one more life, can have such unswerving faith.

Ananda, it is difficult to obtain a human body. If you want to be born as a human, it is very difficult. **It is also difficult to have faith in and to revere the Triple Jewel.** To have genuine faith and reverence for the Buddhas, the Dharma, and the Saṅgha is also very difficult. **It is even more difficult to be able to hear the name of the World Honored One, Medicine Master Vaiḍūrya Light**

Tathāgata. It is even harder to hear the name of Medicine Master Buddha than to do the things mentioned above.

The Buddha calls out again, "**Ananda,** you should know that **Medicine Master Vaiḍūrya Light Tathāgata possesses boundless Bodhisattva practices.** In past lives, he cultivated the immeasurably vast Bodhisattva path, employed **limitless skillful expedients, and** made **immeasurably vast, great vows. If I were to speak extensively of those for** a period of **an eon or more, the eon,** which is such a long period of time, **would soon end, but that Buddha's practices, vows, and skillful expedients have no end!** One could never finish speaking of them."

[Note: End of section lectured by a disciple.]

Sutra:

At that time within the assembly, a Bodhisattva Mahāsattva named One Who Rescues and Liberates arose from his seat, bared his right shoulder, knelt with his right knee on the ground, leaned forward with his palms joined together, and said to the Buddha, "Greatly virtuous World Honored One! During the Dharma Image Age, there will be living beings afflicted with various diseases, emaciated from chronic illnesses, unable to eat or drink, their throats parched and their lips dry. Such a being sees darkness gathering all around him as the signs of death appear. While lying in bed, surrounded by his weeping parents, relatives, and friends, he sees the messengers of Yama leading his spirit before that king of justice. Every sentient being has spirits that stay with him throughout his life. They record his every deed, both good and evil, to present to Yama, the king of justice. At that time, King Yama interrogates this person in order to tally his karma and mete out judgment according to his good and evil deeds.

"At that time, if the sick person's relatives and friends, on his behalf, can take refuge with the World Honored One, Medicine Master Vaiḍūrya Light Tathā-gata, and request members of the Saṅgha to recite this Sutra, to light seven layers of lamps, and to hang up the five-colored banners for prolonging life, then it is possible for his spirit to return. As if in a dream, the person will see everything very clearly himself."

Commentary:

The preceding passage said that even if one were to speak for endless eons, one could hardly finish describing the conduct, vows, and skillful means of Medicine Master Vaiḍūrya Light Tathāgata. **At that time within the assembly, a Bodhisattva Mahāsattva,** a great Bodhisattva among the Bodhisattvas, **named One Who Rescues and Liberates arose from his seat, bared his right shoulder,** and **knelt with his right knee on the ground,** showing respect in body and mind. He **leaned forward with his palms joined together** in single-minded submission **and said to the Buddha, "Greatly virtuous World Honored One!"**

"**During the Dharma Image Age...** When the Proper Dharma Age comes to an end, the world is in the Dharma Image Age. During the Proper Dharma Age, people are strong in *samādhi* and many attain Arhatship. In the Dharma Image Age, people concentrate on making Buddha images and building temples. **There will be living beings** afflicted with various diseases. Beset by all kinds of illnesses, they are never at ease. Emaciated from chronic illness, unable to eat or drink, their throats parched and their lips dry. They are in extreme misery, reduced to skin and bones, yet are unable to take either food or drink. Their throats and lips are terribly parched, but they cannot even swallow water.

Such a being sees darkness gathering all around him as the signs of death appear. He sees no light at all. It is extremely dark and frightening, and he has the constant foreboding that death is at hand. While lying on the bed, surrounded by his weeping parents, close relatives, and friends and good advisors, all of whom are crying piteously, he sees the messengers of King Yama leading his spirit before that king of justice.

Every sentient being has spirits that stay with him throughout his life. They record his every deed, both good and evil, to present to Yama, the king of justice. At that time, the souls of other people who are acquainted with the dying one are also summoned by King Yama. Then the dying one sees everything that he did in his life appear before him. At that time, King Yama interrogates this person, putting him on trial in order to tally his karma, the offenses that he created, and mete out judgment according to the severity of his good and evil deeds.

"At that time, if the sick person's parents, close relatives and friends, on his behalf, can create merit and virtue... If they very earnestly take refuge with the World Honored One, Medicine Master Vaiḍūrya Light Tathāgata, and request members of the Saṅgha, virtuous left-home people who hold the precepts and cultivate, to recite this Sutra, the *Sutra of the Merit and Virtue of the Past Vows of Medicine Master Vaiḍūrya Light Tathāgata*, or to light seven layers of lamps—with seven lamps in each layer, a total of forty-nine lamps—and to hang up the five-colored spiritual banners for prolonging life for his sake, then, it is possible for his spirit to return. If such a Dharma assembly is held, his soul will be able to return. As if in a dream, the person will see everything very clearly himself. He himself sees this kind of state and remembers it.

Sutra:

"If his spirit returns after seven, twenty-one, thirty-five, or forty-nine days, he will feel as if awakened from a dream and will remember the retributions that he underwent for his good and bad karma. Having personally witnessed the retributions of his own karma, he will never again do any evil, even if his very life is endangered. Therefore, good men and women of pure faith should accept and uphold the name of Medicine Master Vaiḍūrya Light Tathāgata and, according to their capability, worship and make offerings to him."

Commentary:

If his spirit returns after seven, twenty-one, thirty-five, or forty-nine days... His friends and relatives recite the Sutra or bow in repentance, hoping to recall his soul from King Yama's realm. After one, three, five, or seven weeks of reciting or repenting, his soul may come back. It's not for sure how long it will take. When the person's soul returns, he will feel as if awakened from a dream and will remember the retributions that he underwent for his good and bad karma. He will remember everything that he experienced. He will remember the good and bad karma that he created, as well as the retributions that they resulted in.

Having personally witnessed the retributions of his own karma, he will never again do any evil, even if his very life is endangered. He has personally seen that every time he creates offenses in delusion, he has to undergo the retribution. Therefore, even if his life is at stake, he will never again commit any offense, great or small. He will not create any more bad karma in the future.

Therefore, good men and women of pure faith, and all living beings in general, should accept and uphold the name of Medicine Master Vaiḍūrya Light Tathāgata, reciting his name, and according to their capability, to the utmost of their strength and ability, worship and make offerings to him.

Sutra:

> At that time, Ananda asked the Bodhisattva Who Rescues and Liberates, "Good man, how should we worship and make offerings to the World Honored One, Medicine Master Vaiḍūrya Light Tathāgata? And how should we make the banners and lamps that prolong life?"
>
> The Bodhisattva Who Rescues and Liberates said, "Greatly Virtuous One, if there is a sick person who wishes to be freed from sickness and suffering, for his sake one should accept and uphold the eight precepts for seven days and seven nights, and make offerings

to the Bhikshu Saṅgha of as many items of food, drink, and other necessities as are in his power to give.

"During the six periods of the day and night one should worship, practice the Way, and make offerings to the World Honored One, Medicine Master Vaiḍūrya Light Tathāgata. Read and recite this Sutra forty-nine times, light forty-nine lamps, and make seven images of that Tathāgata. In front of each image place seven lamps, each as large as a cartwheel. These lamps must be kept burning continuously for forty-nine days. Hang up five-colored banners that are forty-nine spans long. Liberate a variety of living creatures, as many as forty-nine species. Then the sick one will be able to surmount the danger and will not suffer an untimely death or be held by evil ghosts."

Commentary:

At that time, Ananda was still a bit unclear, so he further asked the Bodhisattva Who Rescues and Liberates, "Good man, how should we worship and make offerings to the World Honored One, Medicine Master Vaiḍūrya Light Tathāgata? And how should we make the banners and lamps that prolong life? What are these lamps and banners that prolong life? What is meant by seven layers of lamps? How are the lamps to be placed and lit? How should the life-prolonging banners be made so that they can prolong life?"

The Bodhisattva Who Rescues and Liberates said to Ananda, "Greatly Virtuous One, in the future, if there is a sick person in the Sahā world who wishes to leave behind and be freed from all his sickness and suffering, for his

151

sake one should accept and uphold the eight precepts for seven days and seven nights.

And one should make offerings to the Bhikshu Saṅgha of as many items of food, drink, and other necessities as are in his power to give. You should make offerings in accord with your own capacity. During the six periods of the day and night, one should bow in worship to Medicine Master Buddha, and practice the Way by reciting the *Sutra of the Merit and Virtue of the Past Vows of Medicine Master Vaidūrya Light Tathāgata*, bowing the Medicine Master Repentance, and so forth. And with utmost sincerity, one should make offerings to the World Honored One, Medicine Master Vaidūrya Light Tathāgata, to the extent of one's ability. Read and recite this Sutra forty-nine times, light forty-nine lamps, and make seven images of that Tathāgata.

In front of each image place an offering of seven lamps, each as large as a cartwheel. Since there are seven images, forty-nine lamps are required. How big are they? Cartwheels can be large or small, so the size is not fixed. The most important thing is to be sincere. These forty-nine lamps must be kept burning continuously for forty-nine days. None of the lamps should be allowed to go out. One should frequently add oil to the lamps to make sure that they stay lit.

Hang up five-colored banners that are forty-nine spans long. Make the banners from material of five different colors. Liberate a variety of living creatures, from as many as forty-nine species. The banners should depict an assortment of creatures, such as the twelve animals of the Chinese zodiac. Many species of beings, not just one, are to be depicted and also liberated. There should be forty-nine species, or even more than that number. The animals themselves and the dangers that they suffer should be depicted on the banners.

Then the sick one will be able to surmount the danger and will not suffer an untimely death or be held by evil ghosts. His life will no longer be in danger. He will not be held by enemies, resentful ghosts, ghosts that capture "substitute victims," or other sorts of evil ghosts. Nor will he suffer an untimely death caused by drowning, being burned in a fire, a car collision, a plane crash, a train derailment, a shipwreck, and so forth.

Does anyone have opinions or questions about the principles of the Sutra? Do you have any insights into the Sutra's meaning? We should all bring out our opinions and questions for discussion.

The principles that we study in Buddhism are neither your principles, nor my principles, nor the Buddha's principles. They are the principles of logic and wisdom that everyone should follow. Buddhism is not like certain religions that use faulty reasoning to keep people ignorant and uninformed so that they will accept the tenets of the religion without questioning them.

Buddhism comes from a kind of collective wisdom. What accords with wisdom is the truth, while what does not cannot be practiced. The principles that we are investigating are not imposed from upon high with the purpose of keeping us ignorant and uninformed. Therefore, everyone has the right to speak. Using our wisdom, we should determine which doctrines are correct and which are not. We need to have Dharma-Selecting Vision so that we can judge for ourselves, not just follow the opinions of others. We must develop our own wisdom. Each person should open his "mine of wisdom" and discover his own genuine wisdom.

The wisdom of each Buddha is the same. Also, every Sutra discusses the same basic principles. This Sutra says that we can recite the Sutra and help a sick person get well. If we recite for the sake of a deceased person, that person's soul obtains a small portion of the merit and virtue, while we who recite obtain a much larger portion. The soul of the deceased is able to obtain merit and virtue because this Sutra was spoken by the Buddha and therefore has inconceivable power, which is so great that even science cannot fathom it.

What merit and virtue does the person reciting this Sutra obtain and what are the benefits? There are great benefits. Reciting this Sutra opens your mind and breaks your attachments. The breaking of attachments in itself is boundless merit and virtue. Attachments cause you to become deluded, create offenses, and undergo retribution. As soon as you break through your attachments, all offenses are wiped out. Thus, the Buddha spoke this Sutra as well as all the other teachings in order to destroy attachments. Even the tiniest trace of attachment makes it difficult to attain liberation. But if you break through that tiny trace, you will attain liberation and gain limitless merit and virtue.

You may encourage your friends and relatives to take refuge with Medicine Master Vaiḍūrya Light Tathāgata; however, you may not transmit the Three Refuges to them yourself, because you are not a member of the Saṅgha. To learn from the Buddha, one should study and take refuge with the Dharma. To study the Dharma, one should take refuge with the Saṅgha. The Sutra states very clearly that you must request a member of the Saṅgha to perform the ceremonies, including that of taking refuge with Medicine Master Buddha. When you take refuge, you have to be sincere. Don't think of it as something very ordinary. It's not like eating or getting dressed—ordinary matters that you do casually all the time. If you want to study the Dharma, you have to be respectful. The Dharma is transmitted by the Saṅgha. When the Buddha entered Nirvana, he left the Dharma in the world, entrusting it to the Saṅgha. Therefore, if you want to take refuge with Medicine Master Vaiḍūrya Light Tathāgata, you must formally, with the utmost sincerity, request a Saṅgha member to perform the ceremony. It can't be casual or offhand. It's not as simple as saying, "Oh, I can take refuge by myself." When you go to school, you have to take the classes before you can graduate and receive a diploma. If you study on your own at home, then you cannot receive a diploma from the school.

Disciple: The Sutra said, "Liberate a variety of living creatures, as many as forty-nine species." Does this refer to creatures that people eat?

Venerable Master: Is there any species of living beings that is not subject to human consumption? Are cats not eaten by humans? These days, many people eat the flesh of cats. Are rats not eaten by humans? There are also many people who eat rats. You say ants aren't eaten by humans? Now people eat canned ants! Tell me, what kind of living being is not eaten by humans?

Disciple: I'm very happy to read that the merit of this

155

Sutra can bring back the soul of a person who has already lost consciousness and gone before King Yama. Within Christianity and other religions there are also documented cases in which the soul leaves the body and then returns with very clear recall of everything that happened. They "explain" such phenomena as miracles of God. They say that people who don't believe in God will definitely go to hell. They maintain that the faithful will go to heaven even if they sin, whereas the faithless will go to hell even if they do good. This totally illogical argument has confused many people. I'm really glad to read this Sutra, because it offers a very logical explanation and doesn't try to pull the wool over our eyes.

Venerable Master: Your view is correct. Buddhism encourages people to ask questions and resolve their doubts. It's not a despotic religion that brushes away people's questions, saying, "This is God's will, or this is the Buddha's will. You can't ask about it." That's nonsense. The Buddha himself encouraged people to ask questions. People shouldn't live their entire lives in confusion. Students of Buddhism should become more intelligent and knowledgeable every day. Don't be superstitious; don't believe everything you hear. If you don't develop Dharma-Selecting Vision—the genuine wisdom to distinguish between the Dharma and what is not the Dharma—you will have studied the Dharma in vain. The more you study Buddhism, the more you should understand. Recognize the truth and open up your "mine of wisdom."

Sutra:

"**Furthermore, Ananda, in the case of *kṣatriya* princes**

who are due to be anointed on the crowns of their heads, at a time when calamity arises, such as pestilence among the population, invasion by foreign countries, rebellion within their territories, unusual changes in the stars, a solar or lunar eclipse, unseasonal winds and rains, or prolonged drought, those *ksatriya* princes should bring forth an attitude of kindness and compassion toward all sentient beings and grant amnesty to all prisoners. They should follow the above-mentioned methods to make offerings to that World Honored One, Medicine Master Vaiḍūrya Light Tathāgata. Due to these good roots and the power of that Tathāgata's past vows, the country will be safe and peaceful, the winds and rains will be timely, the crops will ripen, and all sentient beings will be blissful and free of disease. Within this country there will be no violence, nor any *yaksas* or other spirits that harm sentient beings, and all evil omens will vanish."

Commentary:

The merit and virtue of this Sutra is inconceivable. If you recite this Sutra, disasters and evil ghosts will not be able to harm you. **Furthermore, Ananda, in the case of *ksatriya* princes who are due to be anointed on the crowns of their heads...** The *ksatriyas [warrior class]* and Brahmans *[priestly class]* were the upper classes in the ancient class structure of India. Among the *ksatriyas*, there were crown princes, who were ritually anointed on the crowns of their heads when they became kings.

At a time when calamity arises, there may be events

157

such as droughts, floods, fires, severe windstorms, **pestilence among the population,** epidemics of locusts or of deathly, infectious diseases, **invasion by foreign countries, or rebellion within their territories.** There may be subversive factions working against the government.

There may be **unusual changes in the stars,** such as stars becoming abnormally large or taking on a strange appearance, stars disintegrating, or comets coming close to the earth. Such stellar aberrations are the cause of wars, floods, fires, epidemics, and other disasters in the world.

A solar or lunar eclipse. For no apparent reason, the sun or the moon may vanish from view in an eclipse. The sunlight vanishes, or the cool, refreshing light of the full moon disappears and one sees a fiery tinge. The hot sun appears to grow cold, and the cool moon appears to warm up. These are also abnormal phenomena.

Unseasonal winds and rains. The rains and winds come when they are not supposed to. When it rains, it pours; and when the wind blows, it's a huge gale—a hurricane that topples houses. **Or a prolonged drought.** There may be great floods or frequent droughts.

If such disasters happen, **those *kṣatriya* princes** who are due to be anointed as kings should become deeply repentant. They should be like King Tang of the Shang dynasty, who said, "I, Lu, this small child, offer a black bull to the Supreme Sovereign Lord. If I have offenses, my people are not to blame. If my people have offenses, let their offenses rest with me." If the people committed crimes, the king felt he was to blame because he had failed to teach them well. In his appeal to Heaven, King Tang acknowledged his own mistakes.

Those who are to be consecrated as kings **should bring forth an attitude of kindness and compassion toward all sentient beings.** They should reflect, "Why are these disasters happening? It must be because I am lacking in compassion." Then they should **grant amnesty to all prisoners,** including those sentenced to death. **They should follow the above-mentioned methods to make offerings to that World Honored One, Medicine Master Vaiḍūrya Light Tathāgata.**

Due to these good roots gained from making offerings to Medicine Master Vaiḍūrya Light Tathāgata **and the power of that Tathāgata's past vows, the country will be peaceful and safe,** free from trouble, **the winds and rains will be timely.** There is a saying describing this:

> *There's a wind every five days,*
> *And a rain every ten days.*
> *The wind doesn't make the branches cry out,*
> *And the rain doesn't break up the clumps of sod.*

When the wind blows, it doesn't cause the willow branches to make swishing sounds. It doesn't make the trees sound as if they were weeping. "The rain doesn't break up the clumps of sod" means it's a fine drizzle. There is another verse:

> *A fine drizzle gives the streets an oily sheen.*
> *In the distance, you can see the appearance of grass—*
> *And yet, as you walk closer, there's nothing there.*
> *Spring is the best time of the year:*
> *Superb views of misty willows all over the capital.*

The fine drizzle, which is compared to oil, moistens the myriad plants so that they thrive luxuriantly. This kind of rain is so gentle that it doesn't even break up clumps of dirt. It's not a violent storm that topples houses, uproots trees, and injures people.

The winds and rains will be timely, and **the crops will ripen.** There will be abundant harvests of all the various grains. **And all sentient beings will be blissful and free of disease. Within this country there will be no violence.** Murder, arson, robbery, and other violent crimes will be unknown in the land. Such things happen now, unfortunately, because we have been born in a violent age. Our lives are fraught with fear and insecurity. **Nor any** *yakṣas* **or other spirits that harm sentient beings.** *Yakṣas* are "speedy ghosts." No malevolent ghosts or spirits will come to cause trouble, **and all evil omens will vanish.**

Sutra:

> "The *kṣatriya* princes who are due to be anointed on the crowns of their heads will enjoy longer lives and good health, and they will be at ease and free from illness. Ananda, if the queens, the princes, the ministers or court counselors, the ladies of the palace, the provincial officials or the common people suffer from diseases or other difficulties, they should also hang up five-colored spiritual banners, light lamps and keep them burning, liberate living creatures, strew flowers of various colors, and burn precious incense. Then those people will be cured of their diseases and relieved of their difficulties."
>
> Then Ananda asked the Bodhisattva Who Rescues and Liberates, "Good man, how can a life that has come to an end be prolonged?"
>
> The Bodhisattva Who Rescues and Liberates answered, "Greatly Virtuous One, did you not hear

160

the Tathāgata say that there are nine kinds of untimely death? That is why people are exhorted to make life-prolonging banners and lamps and to cultivate all kinds of blessings. Through such cultivation of blessings, they will be freed from suffering and adversity for the rest of their lives."

Commentary:

The *kṣatriya* princes who are due to be anointed on the crowns of their heads will enjoy longer lives and good health, and they will be at ease and free from illness. Ananda, if the queens, the princes, the ministers or court counselors, the ladies of the palace, the provincial officials or the common people suffer from diseases or other difficulties, they should also hang up five-colored spiritual banners, light forty-nine lamps and keep them burning before seven statues of Medicine Master Buddha, as a way to make offerings to him. They should liberate living creatures that were destined for slaughter.

They should also strew flowers of various colors as an offering to that Buddha and burn precious incense, such as aloe-wood incense and *chandana* incense, especially incense of *chandana* wood from Mount Oxhead. Then those people will be cured of their diseases and relieved of their difficulties.

Then Ananda, wishing to request more Dharma on behalf of living beings, asked the Bodhisattva Who Rescues and Liberates, "Good man, how can a life that has come to an end be prolonged? How is it possible that a dying person can extend his life and become healthy again? What's the principle behind this? I don't understand."

The Bodhisattva Who Rescues and Liberates answered, "Greatly Virtuous One, did you not hear the Tathāgata say that there are nine kinds of untimely death? Haven't you heard the Buddha explain that there are nine kinds of death caused by accidents and disasters? Since you have heard it, you will know that **that is why**, in the Buddhist Sutras, all **people are exhorted to make life-prolonging**, five-colored, spiritual **banners and** forty-nine life-prolonging, spiritual **lamps and to cultivate all kinds of blessings. Through** the merit and virtue of **such cultivation of blessings, they will be freed from suffering and adversity for the rest of their lives.** They will not meet with the nine kinds of untimely deaths."

Sutra:

Ananda asked, "What are the nine kinds of untimely death?"

The Bodhisattva Who Rescues and Liberates said, "There may be living beings who, although not seriously ill, have neither medicine nor a doctor to treat them, or else they meet a doctor who gives them the wrong medicine; consequently, they meet with an untimely death. Some of them believe in worldly cults, whose deviant teachers frighten them with false prophecies. Unable to set their minds at ease, they consult oracles to find out what calamities are in store for them. In order to propitiate the spirits, they kill various creatures. They pray to *wang liang* ghosts for aid and protection. Although they wish to prolong their lives, their efforts are to no avail. They deludedly hold to wrong beliefs and perverse views.

Thus they meet with an untimely death and fall into the hells, never to come out. This is the first kind of untimely death."

Commentary:

After **Ananda** heard the Bodhisattva's answer, he said, "Although I have heard this before, will you please explain it for me again in greater detail? That way, living beings of the future can also listen to the explanation." He **asked, "What are the nine kinds of untimely death?"**

The Bodhisattva Who Rescues and Liberates said, "There may be living beings who, although not seriously ill, suffering from only a slight cold, a cough, or some other minor ailment, **have neither medicine nor a doctor to treat them, or else they meet a doctor who gives them the wrong medicine; consequently, they meet with an untimely death.** Perhaps their doctor turns out to be a quack who "cures" them to death by prescribing the wrong medicine. Maybe the doctor prescribes eye medication for a stomach ache, or headache pills for a sore throat. Or perhaps he gives them the wrong injection or performs the wrong operation, so they end up dying earlier than they were supposed to.

Some of them believe in worldly cults whose deviant teachers frighten them with false prophecies. They believe in fortune-tellers, astrologers, geomancers, and so on. The leaders of such deviant cults are actually demons, ghosts, and goblins, who try to alarm people, making false predictions such as: "You'd better not go out for a hundred days, or you might have a car accident!" "Your husband is fooling around on the side, did you know that?" They turn people into nervous wrecks and then tell them, "If you pay me $200,000, I can get you out of trouble."

Unable to set their minds at ease, they consult oracles to find out what calamities are in store for them. These people consult fortune-tellers: "Please take a look at my fortune. Are there any troubles in store for me?" "No problem; three hundred dollars, please!" says the fortune-teller. Ha! Three hundred dollars and your problems will be solved! **In order to propitiate the spirits, they kill various creatures.** The fortune-teller says, "Make a sacrifice of a cat or seven rats, and then I'll report your meritorious deed to King Yama, and he'll pardon your offense."

They pray to *wang liang* ghosts for aid and protection. People pray to the ox-headed and horse-faced ghosts, the *li, mei,* and *wang liang,* for protection and longevity, but actually, these ghosts "protect" them by causing them to die sooner!

Although they wish to prolong their lives, their efforts are to no avail. Their prayers to these ghosts are in vain. **They deludedly hold to wrong beliefs and perverse views.** This is nothing but superstition! They are confused and extremely stupid, with no wisdom at all. **Thus they meet with an untimely death and fall into the hells, never to come out.** They had hoped to live longer, but they only hasten their death. After they die they will fall into the hells forever, because of their extremely deviant beliefs and their wish to lengthen their lives at the expense of others. **This is the first kind of untimely death.**

Sutra:

"The second kind of untimely death is to be executed

at the hands of the law. The third kind is to hunt for sport, to indulge in drinking and lust, or to become excessively dissipated, and then to be waylaid by nonhuman beings that rob one's essence and energy. The fourth is to be burned to death; the fifth is to drown; the sixth is to be devoured by wild beasts; the seventh is to fall from a steep cliff; the eighth is to be harmed by poison, voodoo, evil mantras, or corpse-raising ghosts; the ninth is to die from hunger and thirst. These are the nine kinds of untimely deaths generally spoken of by the Tathāgata. There are also innumerable other kinds which cannot all be spoken of here."

Commentary:

The second untimely kind of death is to be executed at the hands of the law. Law enforcement officials may arrest you without bothering to determine whether the charges against you are true. You are killed regardless of whether you committed the crime. This is a kind of retribution.

The third kind is to hunt for sport. Hunters shoot down deer, birds, or other animals for sport, treating animals as playthings. Some people **indulge in drinking** and **lust,** being promiscuous and not following the rules of propriety. People who drive while intoxicated risk losing their lives in a car accident, which is also a kind of untimely death. Or one may **become excessively dissipated** so that, unable to restrain oneself, one steps beyond the bounds of proper behavior. And then one is **waylaid by nonhuman beings that rob one's essence and energy.** These non-human beings, which refer to *li, mei,* and *wang liang* ghosts, goblins, demons, sprites of the hills and rivers, and other weird beings, consume people's essence and energy as if they were eating vitamins. These unruly and unprincipled beings deprive others of essence and energy in order to prolong their own lives. This is the third kind of untimely death.

The fourth is to be burned to death in a great blaze. Perhaps one's house is set on fire. **The fifth is to drown; the sixth is to be devoured by wild beasts.** One might be torn to pieces by wolves, tigers, or crocodiles, bitten by a snake, or swallowed by a whale. **The seventh is to fall from a steep cliff** and be dashed to pieces on the rocks below.

The eighth is to be harmed by poison, voodoo, evil mantras, or corpse-raising ghosts. There is a practice of witchcraft in which someone makes a straw doll containing a slip of paper with the victim's time and date of birth inside it, and then shoots arrows at the doll for one hundred days, after which time the victim dies. There are evil mantras that can be used to cause the victim to go crazy and try to commit suicide. There are also mantras that cause ghosts to "raise corpses" and make them walk at night. In the eighth kind of untimely death, one is killed by poison, hexes, secret mantras, and so forth.

The ninth is to die of hunger and thirst. Some people suffer from thirst or starvation and eventually die of it. **These are the nine kinds of untimely deaths generally spoken of by the Tathāgata. There are also innumerable other kinds which cannot all be spoken of here.** If one were to go into all the other kinds of accidents and disasters, there would be no end. It would be difficult to explain them all.

Many people in this world undergo the nine kinds of untimely death, because they were not careful to plant good causes. For example, someone may take the wrong medicine in this life because he poisoned someone in a previous life. If one planted the evil cause of cheating others in a past life, one may die from taking the wrong medicine, receiving the wrong shot, getting the wrong surgery, or some other accident in this life.

The second kind of untimely death is to be executed at the hands of the law. The law is supposed to be fair and just, but sometimes people are condemned and put to death without any justifiable grounds.

The third kind of death involves hunting. When hunters go into the woods, the birds and beasts know that their lives are in peril, but they cannot escape. How can we witness their cruel deaths and still consider hunting a sport? How can we justify taking other creatures' lives for our own amusement? When people indulge in drinking and debauchery, their natures become confused. At that point, non-human beings are attracted to them and rob them of their essence and energy, stealing their "gasoline."

In the fourth kind, one is roasted alive because one enjoyed barbecued and roast meat in past lives. If you barbecue others, others will barbecue you!

The fifth kind of death is by drowning, which is the retribution for having drowned beings in past lives. For instance, you may have drowned ants. Maybe I, this tiny ant, drowned in the past because of you! As retribution for drowning others, you get to put yourself in their shoes! You swallow a lot of water until your belly is bloated like a drum, and then you die.

167

The sixth kind of untimely death is to be devoured by wild beasts. Such is the retribution for cruel-hearted connoisseurs of such "delicacies" as "fruit-foxes," monkeys' brains, bears' paws scorched in the fire, or live fish that are still flopping around. These gourmets ate such beings with great relish, so now animals devour their flesh, commenting, "Mmm. Delicious! Your flesh is quite tasty, and your blood isn't bad, either." The animals fight over the gourmets' flesh, making a feast out of them.

The seventh kind of death is to fall over a cliff, which may be a retribution for having robbed others in past lives. Perhaps you found that stealing a person's wallet wasn't enough, so you pushed him over a cliff. I had some classmates who were pushed over a cliff during their school days. Luckily for them, they believed in the Buddha, and so they didn't fall all the way down and were able to climb back up.

The eighth kind is death by poisoning, voodoo, evil mantras, or corpse-raising ghosts. Those who plotted to poison others or control them with hexes in previous lives are themselves poisoned or hexed in this life. As is the cause, so will be the effect. Each kind of karma brings its corresponding retribution. In the practice of witchcraft, a doll is used to represent the victim. The doll may contain a strand of the victim's hair, a piece of their fingernail, or a paper with their birthdate. It may be shot at with arrows, set on fire, or buried, symbolizing the manner of death of the victim. As for corpse-raising ghosts, those who employ mantras to make the ghosts raise corpses may say, "Tonight you must walk one hundred miles. I'll be waiting for you at such-and-such a place." Then, controlled by the mantra, the corpse obediently walks just like a live person for a hundred miles.

The ninth kind is death from hunger, thirst, cold, or heat. In times of famine, starving people laugh hysterically, as if saying, "Do you see me? I'm suffering the retribution for having starved living beings in the past. Don't follow my example!" The law of cause and effect is never off in the slightest. There is nothing unfair about "accidental" deaths; they are simply retribution for past bad karma as determined by the law of cause and effect.

Sutra:

"Moreover, Ananda, King Yama keeps track of the karmic records of all the inhabitants of the world. If there are beings who are not filial to their parents, who commit the Five Rebellious Acts, who revile the Triple Jewel, who destroy the laws of the country, or who violate the precept of truthfulness, then Yama, the king of justice, examines and punishes them according to the severity of their offenses. Therefore, I encourage people to light lamps and make banners, to liberate beings and cultivate blessings so that they can overcome suffering and peril and forestall all disasters."

At that time, twelve great *yakṣa* generals were present in the assembly. They were: General Kumbhīra, General Vajra, General Mihira, General Aṇḍīra, General Anila, General Saṇḍira, General Indra, General Pajra, General Makura, General Kinnara, General Catura, and General Vikarāla.

These twelve great *yakṣa* generals, each with a retinue of seven thousand *yakṣas*, simultaneously raised their voices and addressed the Buddha, "World Honored One! Today, by relying on the Buddha's awesome power, we are able to hear the name of the World Honored One, Medicine Master Vaiḍūrya Light Tathāgata! As a result, we are no longer afraid of the evil destinies. All of us are of one mind to take refuge with the Buddha, the Dharma, and the Saṅgha to the end of our lives. We vow to support all living beings and to benefit them, so that they may live in peace and happiness. In whatever cities, villages, countries, or secluded forests this Sutra circulates, or wherever people accept and uphold the name of Medicine Master Vaiḍūrya Light Tathāgata and venerate and make offerings to him, we, together with our retinues, will guard and protect them, deliver them from all distress, and fulfill all their wishes. If a person wishes to dispel illnesses and difficulties, he should read or recite this Sutra and tie a five-colored thread into knots, forming the letters of our names. He should untie the knots when his wishes have been fulfilled."

Commentary:

"**Moreover, Ananda, King Yama keeps track of the karmic records of all the inhabitants of the world**, both those in the realm of the living and those in the underworld. **If there are beings who are not filial to their parents**, who commit the ten evil deeds and fail to practice the ten good deeds, or **who commit the Five Rebellious Acts...** The Five Rebellious Acts are:

1. Killing one's father
2. Killing one's mother
3. Killing one's teacher (*ācārya*)
4. Destroying the harmony of the Saṅgha
5. Shedding the Buddha's blood

Now that you know that killing your teacher is a rebellious act, I'm sure none of you will dare to murder me! Sometimes the third rebellious act is listed as killing an Arhat—the Arhat is just one's teacher. If the members of the Saṅgha had been dwelling peacefully and happily in the monastery, but you go there and break them up, then you are "destroying the harmony of the Saṅgha." "Shedding the Buddha's blood" includes destroying statues and images of Buddhas and Bodhisattvas. If you break a statue of the Buddha, and it wasn't an accident, you are also shedding the Buddha's blood. If you didn't mean to break it, then it doesn't count as a rebellious act, so don't panic and think you're going to fall into the hells.

Who revile the Triple Jewel: People may slander the Triple Jewel, saying, "The Buddha was superstitious, and so are his followers. The members of the Saṅgha do not really cultivate or hold the precepts. Don't believe in the Sutras; they are inauthentic texts." **Who destroy the laws of the country, or who violate the precept of truthfulness.** Some people encourage others to lie and break the precepts, "Why be honest? If you can cheat and get away with it, go ahead!"

Then Yama, the king of justice, examines and punishes them according to the severity of their offenses. King Yama verifies that they really committed those offenses, and then he punishes them.

171

Therefore, I encourage people to light forty-nine lamps and make long-life banners, to liberate various kinds of beings and cultivate all kinds of blessings so that they can overcome suffering and peril and forestall all disasters."

At that time, twelve great *yakṣa* generals—great generals among the speedy ghosts—were present in the Dharma assembly. They were: General Kumbhīra, General Vajra, General Mihira, General Aṇḍīra, General Anila, General Saṇḍira, General Indra, General Pajra, General Makura, General Kinnara, General Catura, and General Vikarāla.

These twelve great *yakṣa* generals, each with a retinue of seven thousand *yakṣas* at their command, simultaneously raised their voices and addressed the Buddha, "World Honored One! Today, by relying on the Buddha's awesome power, which has drawn us to this Dharma assembly, we are able to hear the name of the World Honored One, Medicine Master Vaiḍūrya Light Tathāgata! As a result, we are no longer afraid of falling into the three evil destinies. All of us are of one mind to take refuge with the Triple Jewel, with the Buddha, the Dharma, and the Saṅgha, to the end of our lives. We vow to support all beings and to benefit them. We will teach and benefit them without asking for any reward. We wish to bring abundant benefit to them, so that they may live in peace and happiness.

In whatever cities, villages, countries, or secluded forests this Sutra circulates, or wherever people accept and uphold and recite the name of Medicine Master Vaiḍūrya Light Tathāgata and venerate and make offerings to him, we, together with our retinues, will guard and protect them, deliver them from all distress, and fulfill all their wishes. If a person wishes to dispel illnesses and difficulties, he should read or recite this Sutra, the *Sutra of the Merit and Virtue of the Past Vows of Medicine Master Vaiḍūrya Light Tathāgata*, and tie a five-colored thread into knots, forming the letters of our names. He should untie the knots when his wishes have been fulfilled."

This is a kind of mantric dharma. Mantras do not necessarily belong to the Esoteric School. The practitioners of the Esoteric School deliberately gave themselves such a name, making it seem as if they are very mysterious. Mantras are a kind of oath or vow, a kind of prayer. A five-colored thread symbolizes the five directions, each of which has a demon associated with it. When the five-colored thread is tied into knots, it brings stability to insecure places. The *yakṣa* generals made a vow that anyone who spelled out their names with knots tied in a five-colored thread would have his wishes fulfilled. Once that happens, he should untie the knots in order to release the spirits that were evoked. One should not be greedy and try to keep the *yakṣa* generals around after they have granted one's wish.

Sutra:

At that time, the World Honored One praised the great *yakṣa* generals, saying, "Good indeed, good indeed, mighty *yakṣa* generals! All of you who want to repay the kindness of the World Honored One, Medicine Master Vaiḍūrya Light Tathāgata, should always

benefit beings and bring peace and happiness to them
in this way."

Commentary:

At that time, after the *yakṣa* generals had vowed to support
Medicine Master Buddha and to repay his kindness, **the
World Honored One,** Sākyamuni Buddha, **praised the
great *yakṣa* generals, saying, "Good indeed, good indeed,
mighty *yakṣa* generals!** It is truly rare for you twelve *yakṣa*
generals to bring forth such vows. **All of you who want to
repay the kindness of the World Honored One, Medicine
Master Vaiḍūrya Light Tathāgata...** Since the twelve of you
have not forgotten that Buddha's kindness and wish to
repay it, you **should always benefit beings and bring
peace and happiness to them in this way.** Never forget
your vows to enable living beings to leave suffering and
attain bliss."

Sutra:

Then Ananda said to the Buddha, "World Honored
One, what should we call this teaching? How should
we uphold it?"

The Buddha told Ananda, "This teaching is called,
'The Merit and Virtue of the Past Vows of Medicine
Master Vaiḍūrya Light Tathāgata.' It is also called
'Twelve Spiritual Generals' Vows to Use Spiritual
Mantras to Benefit Living Beings.' It is also called,
'Eradicating All Karmic Obstacles.' You should
uphold it in this way."

When the Bhagavan had finished speaking, all the
Bodhisattvas Mahāsattvas, great Hearers, kings,

ministers, Brahmans, laypeople, gods, dragons, *yakṣas*, *gandharvas*, *asuras*, *garuḍas*, *kinnaras*, *mahoragas*, humans, and non-human beings, and all the great assembly, on hearing what the Buddha had said, were greatly delighted. They received it with faith and respectfully practiced it.

Commentary:

Then, after Śākyamuni Buddha had praised the twelve *yakṣa* generals, the Venerable **Ananda**, whose name means "Rejoicing," **said to the Buddha, "World Honored One, what should we call this teaching?** What should the title of this Sutra be? What is this Dharma-door? **How should we uphold it?** How should we receive, uphold, read, and recite this Sutra?"

The Buddha compassionately **told Ananda, "This teaching,** this Sutra, **is called, 'The** Sutra of the **Merit and Virtue of the Past Vows of Medicine Master Vaiḍūrya Light Tathāgata.' It is also called, 'Twelve Spiritual Generals' Vows to Use Spiritual Mantras to Benefit Living Beings.'** This Sutra describes how the twelve *yakṣa* generals vow to benefit beings by using "Medicine Master's True Words for Anointing the Crown" to dispel all enmity, hatred, and retribution for evil deeds. **It is also called, 'Eradicating All Karmic Obstacles.' You should uphold it in this way.** You should accept and uphold this Sutra sincerely, for it can remove all karmic hindrances."

When the Bhagavan, the Buddha, **had finished speaking, all the Bodhisattvas Mahāsattvas**—the great Bodhisattvas among all the Bodhisattvas, **the great Hearers**—the great Arhats who cultivated the Four Noble Truths of suffering, accumulation, cessation, and the Way, **the kings, ministers, Brahmans, laypeople** possessing ten kinds of virtue, **the gods, dragons,** *yakṣas, gandharvas, asuras, garuḍas, kinnaras, mahoragas.* These are the eightfold division of ghosts and spirits. **Humans and non-human beings, and all the great assembly, on hearing what the Buddha had said,** which was later set down as this Sutra, **were greatly delighted.** Everyone was happy, and **they received it with faith and respectfully practiced it.** They had no doubts about the Dharma-door that the Buddha had spoken, and they practiced it throughout their lives.

This concludes the general explanation of the *Sutra of the Merit and Virtue of the Past Vows of Medicine Master Vaiḍūrya Light Tathāgata.* Now everyone should bring up their own opinions. Let's share our ideas and wisdom. You shouldn't only listen to me. Bring up your own ideas, or any questions you have.

Medicine Master Buddha (also known as Akṣobhya Buddha) and Amitābha Buddha are the two Buddhas in the East and the West, respectively. One heads the Vajra Division, and the other, the Lotus Division. The Vajra Division represents the Dharmas of Subduing, subduing living beings by means of joy and giving; the Lotus Division represents the Dharmas of Gathering In, which employ kindness and compassion to gather in all beings.

Why is the Vajra Division associated with joy and giving? When the Buddha subdues heavenly demons and externalists, he doesn't use anger. Rather, practicing joy and giving, he teaches living beings from the opposite side and causes them to renounce the deviant and return to the proper so that they can end birth and death. He gathers them in with kindness and compassion, and subdues them with joy and giving. That's how the Buddha uses the Four Limitless Minds (kindness, compassion, joy, and giving) to teach and transform living beings. Vajra spirits may appear to have fierce and angry eyes, yet in their hearts they practice joy and giving. Bodhisattvas keep their gaze down, which means that they don't get angry. Amitābha Buddha doesn't lose his temper at living beings, but always welcomes them with kindness and compassion.

In the *Daily Recitation Manual of the Chan School*, the "Mantra of the Two Buddhas" says, "Two Buddhas proclaim and transform in the Sahā world—Akṣobhya in the East, Amitābha in the West. If one transgresses any of the thirteen major *pārājika* precepts and is afraid of King Yama, one should diligently repent and reform, and one's offense will be eradicated." Although such an offense is basically unpardonable, if you sincerely repent and reform, it can be eradicated. The "Mantra of the Two Buddhas" is one of the "Dharmas of Hooking and Summoning." When someone has a sickness caused by a ghost, this mantra can be used to summon the ghost. Although the mantra is very efficacious, very few people know how to recite it, and even fewer know how to really use it.

There is also the Pu'an Mantra, which is a Subduing Dharma. Patriarch Pu'an was a former butcher who gave up butchering to cultivate the Way. He transformed his twelve butcher knives into flying knives. When the Pu'an Mantra is recited, his butcher knives fly through the air and frighten all the demons and externalists.

"Medicine Master's True Words for Anointing the Crown" are also part of the Mantra of the Two Buddhas.

These True Words can neutralize all poisons and eradicate all offenses. If you sincerely recite them for a person who has been poisoned, it will neutralize the poison. But it won't work if you recite casually. This mantra is a very important part of the Sutra. When you don't have time to recite the whole Sutra, you can just recite the True Words. It is a short but indispensable Dharma. This Sutra is also called the *Sutra for Eradicating All Karmic Obstacles*. Now that we have learned about this method of practice, we should constantly recite the Medicine Master Mantra, so that we will be safe from disasters and so our good roots will grow.

We should all take turns speaking the Dharma. I shouldn't be the only speaker. I would like to listen to all of you, especially the elders. Although this has not been done before in America, we should all advance in our study of Buddhism. We should all take turns lecturing and sharing our experiences, so that everyone comes away with much more; then we will be able to understand the inconceivable states of Buddhism. Don't be nervous; we're all one big family. Just be candid and talk about your experiences in the Way-place. Relax and feel at ease, and then you'll be able to perceive the wonders of the Buddhadharma.

This world is full of suffering and evil. In the *Amitābha Sutra,* it is called the Evil World of the Five Turbidities. The Five Turbidities are the turbidity of the eon, the turbidity of views, the turbidity of afflictions, the turbidity of living beings, and the turbidity of life spans. The *turbidity of the eon* refers to these impure, defiled times. Since time is defiled, space also becomes defiled and there is air pollution. Breathing the polluted air, sentient beings become polluted as well. It's hard to keep things clean in such a polluted atmosphere. It's difficult to clean up the air, which is suffused with noxious vapors. The atmosphere is heavy and lifeless. There is no peace or happiness anywhere. The energies of violence, terror, murder, arson, robbery, and theft fill the air, poisoning people and causing them to go insane. The few sane ones who are left find no happiness, either. Living in this world, they pass the days as if drunk or dreaming, not knowing what they are doing.

The *turbidity of views*: Since space and time are polluted, what we see and hear is also unclean. We see people committing murders, setting fires, robbing or stealing from others, taking and dealing drugs, gambling, watching pornographic movies, and so on. These things pollute our views until we no longer know what is good. We get carried away by the depraved trends of the world.

Then we become afflicted, thus bringing about the *turbidity of afflictions*. Nothing goes the way we wish. Every situation is aggravating. Seeing some people win fortunes at the casino and forgetting that there are always many more losers than winners, we start gambling as well. The more money we lose, the more we gamble, hoping to win it back. When we have squandered everything, that's when we *really* get afflicted!

Perhaps we notice all the flourishing businesses and decide to start our own business. When our business loses money, we complain, "All the other businesses are making a profit. God, why don't you help me out and let me make some money?" Once we become afflicted, we gripe at everyone, including God. The more afflicted we become, the more troubles we have. "What an unlucky life!" we think.

When God and the other deities don't respond to our

complaints, we direct our anger towards living beings and stir up trouble in the community, bringing the *turbidity of living beings* into being. We end up having no affinities with people. Our relationships with others are impure. As a result, our life is a disaster and the *turbidity of a life span* comes right along.

That's an explanation of the Evil World of Five Turbidities in worldly terms. The five turbidities bring us all kinds of troubles. Although we speak of five turbidities in general, each turbidity contains infinitely many turbidities and we could never describe them all. The Buddha, seeing the endless suffering, confusion, affliction, and strife of beings in the Sahā world, felt that life was totally meaningless.

The Buddha had grown up in the royal palace as the crown prince of a king in an Indian state. One day, the young prince decided to go out the eastern gate of the palace, accompanied by his attendant. When they got outside, he saw a very strange sight: a woman was giving birth, and as soon as the baby was born, it opened its mouth and bawled, "Ku, ku, ku!" *["Ku" means suffering in Chinese.]*

"Why is the baby acting like that?" the prince asked.

His attendant explained, "When birth occurs, the mother bleeds and the baby cries."

The prince immediately lost interest in his walk. "This is no fun," he said. "Let's go back!" And so the trip outside the eastern gate came to an end.

After he returned home, he thought, "There was a crying baby at the eastern gate. Tomorrow I'll try the southern gate." The next day, he went out through the southern gate and saw an old man with wrinkled skin and white hair, who walked with a faltering gait. His teeth had fallen out, his ears were going deaf, and his eyes could not see clearly. He was a pitiful sight. The prince asked his attendant, "What's wrong with him? How did he get this way?" The prince had never seen anyone like that before.

His attendant replied, "That man is so old that his body doesn't help him out anymore. His eyes, ears, and nose have all failed him. Although his tongue still works, it's difficult to eat because he doesn't have any teeth and cannot chew his food. Every part of his body is on strike. His hands can't pick things up, and his legs can hardly support him. His hair is white and his back is hunched."

"What misery!" The prince changed his mind about taking a walk and went back.

On the third day, the prince went out through the western gate. Coming upon a hospital, he walked in and saw many people lying in bed and crying out in agony. Appalled at the sight, the prince returned to the palace.

The next day, he decided to take a look outside the northern gate. When he got there, he saw a mortuary, where they also sold coffins.

"What are those for?" he asked, pointing at the coffins.

"For holding dead bodies," they told him.

In the mortuary, the prince noticed a lot of people lying there with their eyes closed and not breathing—they were corpses. He was even more disillusioned than before.

"What meaning is there to life if we have to undergo the sufferings of birth, old age, sickness, and death?" he wondered.

At that point, the god Vaiśravaṇa [the Heavenly King

who guards the North] manifested as a Bhikshu dressed in ragged robes.

"Who is this?" asked the prince.

"Why don't you ask him?" his attendant said.

"What do you do?" the prince asked the monk.

"I'm a Bhikshu."

"What do you do as a Bhikshu?"

"A Bhikshu's goal is to put an end to the sufferings of birth, old age, sickness, and death," said the monk.

"That sounds good to me," said the prince. "You say you can end birth and death? I would like to try it out, too." Then the prince left the home-life and become a Bhikshu.

He renounced his kingdom and home and went into the Himalayas, where he cultivated ascetic practices for six years, eating only one sesame seed and one grain of wheat each day. In his quest for enlightenment, he suffered what others could not suffer, ate what others could not eat, and practiced what others could not practice. He bore what others could not bear and yielded what others could not yield. He gave up the king's throne and withstood the hunger of eating only one sesame seed and one grain of wheat each day. With that kind of patience and renunciation, he realized Buddhahood. Even though he had been a crown prince, he wanted to cultivate the Way. None of us are in such an honored position. What is there that we still can't bear to give up? Although we can't bear to renounce anything now, when it comes time to die, we won't be able to take anything with us. The prince renounced his kingdom, family, and external possessions and went to cultivate in the mountains. In the beginning, he was accompanied by five people: two trusted relatives on his father's side and three on his mother's side. His parents sent them not to prevent their son from cultivating, but to make sure he was safe from mishap.

When the prince began eating one sesame seed and one grain of wheat a day, two of his five guardians couldn't take the suffering and left. The other three sincerely suffered along with him. The prince was reduced to skin and bones, yet he did not die. When a heavenly maiden offered him some porridge with milk, the prince accepted because he felt obligated to accept any sincere offering, and also because he was famished.

When his three guardians saw this, they said, "Hey, how do you expect to become a Buddha that way? It takes bitter cultivation to realize Buddhahood, yet you're eating porridge! That's it! We're leaving!" And so they also went away. The five guardians all went to the Deer Park.

Think about it: even with his merit and virtue, the future Buddha had to go through such ordeals. At that point, the prince brought forth the Bodhi resolve. When he was meditating in the mountains, he had probably taken an occasional stroll to enjoy the scenery. When his five guardians abandoned him, if he had been like most people, he would have thought, "I might as well return to the palace. What am I putting myself through all this suffering for?" Yet he didn't go back. Instead, he walked to the Bodhi tree and sat down beneath it, vowing, "If I don't become a Buddha, I will never rise from here. I will sit here till I die!"

After that, he sat in meditation for seven weeks. We sit for thirty-five minutes and then cry out, "Aii! The pain in my legs is killing me!" Yesterday, one of my disciples was sitting and meditating on the topic "Be as if dead." How-

183

ever, he still couldn't take it. The Buddha sat for forty-nine days without getting up or eating or drinking anything. Despite his hunger and thirst, he just kept sitting. Just think of the Buddha's vigor in cultivating the Way—would we be able to make such a great resolve for Bodhi?

One night, the prince saw a star in the sky and suddenly became enlightened. He completely fathomed the truths of life and of the universe. Upon his enlightenment, the Buddha exclaimed, "Strange, strange, strange indeed! All beings have the wisdom and virtue of the Tathāgata; all can become Buddhas. It is only because of random thinking and attachments that they cannot certify to this." All living beings possess the Buddha-nature. They all have the Buddha's thirty-two features and eighty subsidiary characteristics. They are all adorned with ten thousand virtues of a Buddha. It is only because of random thinking that they haven't realized Buddhahood. We don't need to learn a lot of Buddhadharma. One sentence is enough: "It is only because of random thinking and attachments that they cannot certify to this."

Our random thoughts suddenly take us up to the heavens and just as suddenly bring us back down to earth. We think about the affairs of the country, our boyfriends and girlfriends, our parents, children, brothers and sisters. We are incredibly busy during the day, and at night we are busy dreaming. In our dreams, we see so many things and people mixed up together that we end up utterly bewildered. Still, we can't put down our attachments. Where do dreams come from? Attachments. If we want to leave distorted dream-thinking far behind, we have to break our attachments.

184

A person of the utmost virtue has no dreams and no random thoughts. He is a sage, a "living dead man," different from ordinary people. Having eliminated all attachments and random thoughts, he realizes Buddhahood. Thus, "it is only because of random thinking and attachments that they cannot certify to this." We should remember this sentence and get rid of our random thoughts and attachments. Once we sweep them away, we will leave dream-thinking far behind and attain ultimate Nirvana!

After the Buddha became enlightened, he wondered which living being he should save first. "Oh, so the Buddha also had a random thought," you say. You can't judge the state of a sage with your ordinary mind. The Buddha wasn't having random thoughts. He was using his Wonderful Contemplative Wisdom to see who was ready to receive his teaching.

Making use of his Wonderful Contemplative Wisdom, he saw that his five former guardians had nearly perfected their cultivation. A few words from the Buddha, or even just the sight of the Buddha, would suffice to bring them to enlightenment. Although they had abandoned the prince before, they were nevertheless deeply influenced by him. They were determined to liberate themselves from birth and death; they cared nothing for worldly wealth, honor, and glory. When they had left the prince, they probably figured, "We can cultivate and become enlightened first, and then we'll help the Prince become enlightened as well." However, none of this is recorded in history books. This is just my own conjecture. They probably thought: "We're spending so much time looking after the Prince that we can't concentrate on our own practice. We ought to go away to work hard on our own cultivation first, and then come back and help the Prince cultivate." Since they had wanted to help the prince, upon achieving Buddhahood he went to enlighten them first. As one sows, so shall one reap.

Contemplating with his Wonderful Contemplative Wisdom, the Wisdom of Accomplishment, the Wisdom of Equality, and the Great Perfect Mirror Wisdom, the Buddha saw that the Venerable Ajñātakauṇḍinya would be the first to become enlightened. And so the Buddha went to save Ajñātakauṇḍinya first, fulfilling a vow that he had made long, long ago.

Limitless eons ago, Ajñātakauṇḍinya had been King Kali, and Śākyamuni Buddha had been a Patient Immortal who cultivated in the mountains. One day King Kali went hunting in the mountains, taking his concubines with him. While the King was hunting, the concubines wandered off and discovered the Patient Immortal. They gathered around him, drawn by his virtue and by their deep affinities with him.

When King Kali, returning in a bad mood from an unsuccessful hunt, saw his concubines gathered around a long-haired, long-nailed, and long-bearded stranger, he immediately grew jealous.

"What are you doing here?" the King demanded of the stranger.

"I'm cultivating the skill of patience," replied the Patient Immortal.

"Patience? What do you mean by seducing my concubines like this? You're certainly up to no good." Drawing his sword, the King promptly hacked off the cultivator's hands and feet, and then asked him if he was angry.

"I'm not angry," said the Patient Immortal.

"I don't believe you," said King Kali. "How could anyone not be angry after their hands and feet had been chopped off. You're lying! What proof do you have that you're not angry?"

The Patient Immortal said, "If I'm not angry, then my hands and feet will grow back again. If I am, then they won't."

When the Patient Immortal finished speaking, his hands and feet did grow back. Seeing that, the King thought, "This must be a monster," and prepared to set the mountain ablaze. But by that time the Dharma-protecting spirits were enraged, and they pelted a shower of hail-stones upon the King.

The Patient Immortal took pity on him and said, "In the future when I become a Buddha, I will first save this person who chopped off my hands and feet." As a result of that vow, when he became Śākyamuni Buddha, he contemplated the causes and effects of his past and present lives and knew that he should first save Ajñātakauṇḍinya and the other four cultivators. Then the Buddha left the Bodhi tree and walked to the Deer Park to look for his five former guardians.

The Deer Park had a large deer population. In past reincarnations, the Buddha had also been a deer king who taught deer. After becoming a Buddha, he taught people. Finding the five cultivators in the Deer Park, the Buddha turned the Dharma-wheel for the first time. He spoke for them the Four Noble Truths of suffering, accumulation, the Way, and cessation. On the first turning, he said, "This is suffering; it is oppressive." Life is filled with suffering. There are the Three Sufferings, the Eight Sufferings, and the limitless sufferings. Mentally and physically oppressed by all these sufferings, living beings never find any peace, happiness, or comfort. These oppressive sufferings dominate their lives.

The Three Sufferings:

1. The suffering within suffering
2. The suffering of decay
3. The suffering of process

The "suffering within suffering" means that in the midst of suffering, there is still more suffering. One has neither food, clothes, nor shelter. That's suffering piled on top of suffering, suffering that never comes to an end.

If one does not undergo the "suffering within suffering" that comes with poverty, one may undergo the "suffering of decay" experienced by rich people when they lose all their wealth in a sudden and unexpected disaster, such as robbery, fire, or flood.

"I'm neither poor nor rich, so these two sufferings don't apply to me," you say.

However, you cannot escape the "suffering of process." From youth until the prime of life, and then on into old age and death, your thoughts flow in an unending succession. That's known as the suffering of process. The life process itself entails suffering.

There are also the Eight Sufferings:

1. The suffering of birth
2. The suffering of old age
3. The suffering of sickness
4. The suffering of death

5. The suffering of being apart from those you love
6. The suffering of being together with those you hate
7. The suffering of not obtaining what you seek
8. The suffering of the raging blaze of the five *skandhas*

Birth is a very uncomfortable experience. You feel as if you were being squeezed between two mountains. You feel as much pain as a live turtle whose shell is ripped off. After a painful birth, you gradually get old. Old age is also suffering. One by one, your organs start failing, and even simple tasks become very difficult. The pain of sickness is even harder to bear. You may moan and cry, but no one can suffer in your stead.

Such suffering is very democratic: everyone from the king down to the lowliest beggar must bear it. Even the emperor, who owns the empire and is worshipped by all—even after his death—suffers just like anyone else when he gets sick. Of course, if you don't get sick, then it's not a problem. If you do, then sickness treats you the same as anyone else; it's not polite at all.

These first three sufferings are still not that bad. The worst suffering is that of death. In the battle between life and death, you want to live, but the Spirit of Death is determined to pull you over to the side of death. The pain of dying is like that of a cow being flayed alive.

Ordinary people have deep emotional attachments. They hope their loved ones will live and their enemies will die. When two people fall in love, they forget about everything else. Like besotted fools, they are always stuck to each other, as if with Crazy Glue, and nothing can pull them apart.

Some of you don't believe what I'm saying. Let me give you an example. You may have seen newspapers report on the birth of Siamese twins in various parts of the world. They are born with their bodies joined together and have to be separated surgically. Just think how painful that is! That's the suffering of being separated from those one loves. In their deep love, they made vows, "In heaven may we be like two birds tied to the same wing, and on earth may our roots intertwine." That's one reason they turned into Siamese twins.

There is also a less pleasant explanation. These Siamese twins were homosexual couples in their past lives. Their appearance actually teaches Dharma for homosexuals. Homosexuals are people who fall in love with those of the same sex. Isn't that confused? Since they cannot bear to be separated from each other, they are reborn as Siamese twins who must be cut apart at birth. See how cruel people are! They see the twins joined together and, out of jealousy, want to separate them, saying, "You can't be this way! You won't be able to live!" One could also see it as compassion: Seeing that the twins can't survive that way, people want to help them by separating them. The compassionate doctor very carefully cuts them apart. See, this world is full of troubles. Siamese twins were very uncommon several decades ago. But with the recent rise in homosexuality, they have been appearing in every country.

Before, a woman might give birth to twins, but they wouldn't be joined together. Probably their love wasn't as muddled; it wasn't as if they'd been glued together with Crazy Glue. People who are so much in love that they can't bear to be separated may end up as Siamese twins. Even then, they can't stay together, because the doctor will separate them surgically. It's a risky operation, and sometimes both twins end up dying. The twins probably think, "If we can't be together, then we don't want to live." They don't want the "suffering of being apart from those one loves."

There is also the suffering of being together with those one hates. "I really detest that person," you think. "The mere sight of him upsets me." You wish to get away from him, but strangely enough, he follows you wherever you go and always makes a point of greeting you and working with you. You detest him, but he always hangs around you! You can't escape him.That's the suffering of being with those whom one hates.

Then there's the suffering of not obtaining what you seek. When you fail to obtain what you seek, you may become so afflicted that you can't sleep at night and you lose your appetite. You feel restless and ill at ease. That's the suffering of not obtaining what you seek.

The worst suffering is that of the raging blaze of the five *skandhas*. The five *skandhas* are form, feeling, thinking, formations, and consciousness. No one can leave them behind. They are so powerful that they have suffocated us and smothered our Buddha-nature. However, once we understand them, we'll see that there's no real substance to them. They are just like clouds drifting by. Once we "illuminate the five *skandhas* and see that they are all empty," as the line from the *Heart Sutra* says, then we know that "originally there was not a single thing; where can the dust alight?" *[from the Sixth Patriarch's verse]*

Let's examine ourselves with regard to suffering. Is there anyone who is free from suffering?

"I am," you say. "I don't have the three sufferings or the eight sufferings. I don't have even a single suffering!" If you claim to have no suffering, you are just trying to fool yourself!

Let me say one more thing. The suffering of "not obtaining what you seek" is very similar to the sufferings of "being together with those you hate" and "being apart from those you love." For example, it's very hard to bear when you fail in your efforts to obtain a high position in the government. If you wish to make a fortune or to become famous, but fail no matter how hard you work, it's also suffering. If you can't find a boyfriend or a girlfriend, that's even more suffering. It's so much suffering that you can't sleep and you don't feel like eating. There have been lovesick fools ever since ancient times. Some are even driven to commit suicide! Isn't that suffering? These are the deluded attachments of worldly people. They take thieves to be their sons and regard suffering as happiness. The harder something is to obtain, the more they covet it. But once it is theirs, they see it as worthless.

For example, young people may hear that a certain kind of drug can make them enlightened. Twenty years ago, LSD was very popular in America. Now marijuana is the most popular drug. Young people are curious and want to experiment with drugs. Those who are able to obtain them become addicted, while those who can't wonder what they are like.

"Can it really make you enlightened?" they wonder. "Does smoking marijuana make you feel as if you were in the heavens?" With their never-ending curiosity and love for new things, they end up harming themselves. Without realizing it, they run right into the world of drugs. Drugs are as sweet as candy to them. They love the "high" that drugs give them and wouldn't trade it for anything. What delusion and suffering!

Although we say there are Eight Sufferings, if we were to go into detail, we could talk about infinite varieties of suffering. The Buddha perceived such suffering and spoke the First Truth of Suffering: "This is suffering; it is oppressive." We should realize how oppressed by suffering people are.

The Buddha then spoke the Second Truth of Accumulation: "This is accumulation; it is incurred." What is accumulated? Afflictions. Perceiving the suffering of living beings, the Buddha vowed to save them. Seeing afflictions being accumulated, he vowed to cut off afflictions. He made these vows:

Living beings are boundless; I vow to save them.
Afflictions are endless; I vow to cut them off.

As the result of the causes one plants, one incurs the accumulation of afflictions. We say there are 84,000 kinds of afflictions, but the number 84,000 actually represents an infinite number.

The Buddha then spoke the Third Truth of the Way: "This is the Way; it can be cultivated." The Bodhi Way—the path to wisdom, to Buddhahood, to ending birth and death, and to leaving suffering and attaining bliss--can be cultivated. You can attain the Way only through cultivation. The next vows are:

Dharma-doors are limitless; I vow to study them.
The Buddha Way is unsurpassed; I vow to realize it.

193

Finally, the Buddha spoke the Fourth Truth of Cessation: "This is cessation; it can be realized." Cessation refers to the bliss of quiescence.

> *All things are impermanent,*
>   *coming into being and ceasing to be.*
> *When coming into being and ceasing to be*
>   *both stop, there is blissful quiescence.*

In the past, Śākyamuni Buddha offered up his life for half of this four-line verse. How did it happen? When he was cultivating in a past life, he met a being from the Heaven of Pure Dwelling who manifested as a *rākṣasa* ghost to test the Buddha's sincerity. The *rākṣasa* ghost walked by the old cultivator chanting to himself, "All things are impermanent, coming into being and ceasing to be."

The cultivator thought, "What's he singing? Oh, it's a verse." Then he asked the ghost, "Hey, what did you just say?"

"I said, 'All things are impermanent, coming into being and ceasing to be.'" replied the ghost.

"Aren't there two more lines to your verse?"

"Yes," said the ghost.

"Please tell me what they are."

"I'm starving, I don't have any energy," said the ghost. " If you give me something to eat, I'll tell you."

"Okay," said the Buddha. "I'll offer you whatever you want, and then you can tell me those two lines."

The *rākṣasa* ghost said, "I need to eat the flesh and drink the blood of a living human being. Can you give up your own flesh and blood?"

The Buddha thought, "Well, if I get to hear the Dharma, then my death will be worth it. But if I don't get to hear those two lines of verse, I'll never be able to put everything down." And so the Buddha replied, "Fine, tell me the rest of the verse, and then I'll let you eat me."

"Okay," said the ghost. "The last two lines are: 'When coming into being and ceasing to be both stop, there is blissful quiescence.' Everything in the world is impermanent, coming into being and ceasing to be. The attainment of what neither comes into being nor ceases to be is true and eternal happiness. Okay, now I'm going to eat you."

"Hold on!" said the cultivator. "Don't eat me yet!"

"What? Are you going back on your promise?"

"No, no, I'm not going back on my promise. I just want to carve this verse on a tree, so it will remain in the world. When people see it, they will bring forth the Bodhi mind and eventually attain the Way."

"That sounds like a good idea," the *rākṣasa* ghost said. "Go ahead and carve it."

The cultivator scraped off the outer bark of a tree with a knife and carved the verse onto the tree. Meanwhile, the *rākṣasa* began wailing, "Please hurry! I'm really famished!"

After the cultivator quickly finished carving, the *rākṣasa* said, "I'm not going to be polite anymore. I must eat your flesh and drink your blood."

"Hold on," said the cultivator. "Please wait a bit longer."

"What? You've taken so long already—what else do you want to do?" complained the ghost.

The cultivator said, "The words on the tree will eventually be worn away by the elements. I want to chisel this verse in stone so that it will last forever. Please be patient for a little while longer as I do this."

195

"Oh, alright!" said the *rākṣasa*.

When the cultivator finished chiseling, the *rākṣasa* said, "Now I can eat you!"

"Fine," said the cultivator, as he closed his eyes and waited to be eaten.

Suddenly a voice in space said, "Bravo! You are a true cultivator who is able to sacrifice himself for the Dharma. You will certainly become a Buddha." When the cultivator opened his eyes, the *rākṣasa* ghost was gone and a god from the Heaven of Pure Dwelling appeared before him.

That is known as "not being afraid to renounce one's life for half a verse." Could we be that sincere in our study of Buddhism? Could we renounce our lives for half a verse or for a Sutra?

There are still many people in this world who wish to cultivate. At the City of Ten Thousand Buddhas, we encourage everyone to recite, study, and memorize the *Śūraṅgama Sūtra*. Some people have studied two or three rolls of the Sutra, but no one has memorized the whole Sutra yet. A month before Amitābha Buddha's anniversary, someone vowed to go into seclusion for one month and memorize the *Earth Store Sutra* and the *Brahma Net Sutra*. I gave her permission and asked someone to be her attendant, providing her with food and water and aiding her to fulfill her vow. By the end of the month, she was able to recite both the *Earth Store Sutra* and the *Brahma Net Sutra* from memory. She is the first person at the City of Ten Thousand Buddhas to memorize these two Sutras. I won't tell you her name, because I don't want to give her publicity. Most of the cultivators at the City have resolves similar to hers. Recently, an acupuncturist from Los Angeles also went into seclusion for ten days at the City and memorized the *Vajra Sutra.*

"The Way can be cultivated. Cessation can be realized." The bliss of quiescence can be realized by anyone who truly cultivates. Once you recognize suffering, you can halt the accumulation of afflictions. Yearning for the bliss of still extinction, you cultivate the Way. This is called "knowing suffering, ending accumulation, yearning for cessation, and cultivating the Way."

On the first turning of the Dharma-wheel, the Buddha said:

This is suffering; it is oppressive.
This is accumulation; it is incurred.
This is the Way; it can be cultivated.
This is cessation; it can be realized.

The original order was "suffering, accumulation, the Way, and cessation." However, the Chinese changed it to be "suffering, accumulation, cessation, and the Way," because it sounds smoother that way.

On the second turning, the Buddha said: *This is suffering; I already know it. I don't need to know it further.* I already know suffering, and I don't want to undergo it anymore. I don't want to know more about suffering. *This is accumulation. I have already cut it off. I don't need to cut it off further.* I have no further afflictions. *This is the Way. I have already cultivated it.* I have already cultivated the Bodhi Way and accomplished Buddhahood. *This is cessation. I have already realized it.* I have completely understood the Dharma of suffering, accumulation, cessation, and the Way.

197

On the third turning the Buddha said:

This is suffering; you should know it.
This is accumulation; you should cut it off.
This is the Way; you should cultivate it.
This is cessation; you should realize it.

When the Buddha had spoken the three turnings of the Dharma-wheel of the Four Noble Truths, the Venerable Ajñātakauṇḍinya immediately realized Arhatship. Now that we have heard the three turnings, has anyone realized Arhatship?

End of the explanation of the *Sutra of the Merit and Virtue of the Past Vows of Medicine Master Vaiḍūrya Light Tathāgata.*

Biographical Sketch of the Venerable Master Hsuan Hua

The Venerable Master, a native of Shuangcheng County in Jilin Province of China, was born on the sixteenth day of the third lunar month in the year of *wuwu* at the beginning of the century. He was named Yushu (or Yuxi) Bai. His father, Fuhai Bai, was hardworking and thrifty. His mother, maiden name Hu, ate only vegetarian food and recited the Buddha's name every day. When she was pregnant with the Master, she prayed to the Buddhas and Bodhisattvas. The night before his birth, in a dream she saw Amitabha Buddha emitting brilliant light. Following that the Master was born.

The Master was quiet and untalkative by nature, but he had a righteous and heroic spirit. As a child, he followed his mother's example and ate only vegetarian food and recited the Buddha's name. At the age of eleven, the sight of a dead infant made him aware of the great matter of birth and death, and he resolved to leave the home-life. At twelve, he heard of how Filial Son Wong (Great Master Chang Ren) of Shuangcheng County had practiced filial piety and attained the Way, and he vowed to follow the Filial Son's example. The Master decided to bow to his parents every morning and evening as a way of acknowledging his faults and repaying his parents' kindness. Because of his filial piety, he became known as Filial Son Bai.

At fifteen, he took refuge under the Venerable Master Chang Zhi. That year he began to attend school and mastered the Four Books, the Five Classics, the texts of various Chinese schools of thought, and the fields of medicine, divination, astrology, and physiognomy. He participated in the Virtue Society and other charitable societies. He explained the *Sixth Patriarch's Sutra*, the *Vajra Sutra*, and other Sutras to those who were illiterate, and he started a free school for the poor.

When he was nineteen, his mother passed away, and he requested Venerable Master Chang Zhi of Sanyuan (Three Conditions) Monastery to shave his head. He was given the Dharma name An Tse and style name To Lun. Dressed in the left-home robes, he built a simple hut by his mother's grave and lived there for three years in observance of filial piety. During that period, he made eighteen great vows (see page 206). He bowed to the *Flower Adornment Sutra*, engaged in worship and repentance, practiced meditation, studied the scriptures, ate only one meal a day, and did not lie down to sleep at night. His sincere efforts to purify and cultivate himself won the admiration of the villagers and evoked numerous miracles and responses from the Buddhas, Bodhisattvas, and Dharma-protecting gods and dragons. He came to be known as an extraordinary monk.

One day as he was sitting in meditation, he saw the Great Master, the Sixth Patriarch, come to his hut and tell him, "In the future you will go to the West and meet countless people. The living beings you teach and transform will be as countless as the sands of the Ganges River. That will mark the beginning of the Buddhadharma in the West." After saying that, the Sixth Patriarch vanished. The

Master completed his observance of filial piety and went to Changbai Mountain, where he dwelled in seclusion and practiced austerities at the Amitabha Cave. Later he returned to Sanyuan Monastery and became the leader of the assembly. During his years in Manchuria, the Master taught people according to their potentials. He awakened those who were confused and saved many lives. Countless dragons, snakes, foxes, ghosts, and spirits took refuge and received the precepts from him, changing their evil and cultivating goodness.

In 1946, the Master embarked on an arduous journey to Caoxi, Guangzhou, to pay homage to the Elder Master Hsu Yun, whom he esteemed as a great hero of Buddhism. Along the way he stayed at many renowned monasteries in China and received complete ordination at Mount Putuo in 1947. He reached Nanhua Monastery in 1948 and paid homage to Elder Master Hsu Yun. The Elder Master appointed him as an instructor and later as the Dean of Academic Affairs in the Nanhua Vinaya Academy. He saw that the Master was an outstanding individual and transmitted the Dharma to him, giving him the Dharma name Hsuan Hua and making him the Ninth Patriarch of the Wei Yang Sect, the forty-fifth generation since the First Patriarch Mahakashyapa.

In 1949, the Master bid farewell to the Elder Master Yun and went to Hong Kong. In propagating the Dharma there, he emphasized all five schools of Buddhism—Chan, Doctrine, Vinaya, Esoteric, and Pure Land. He renovated old temples, printed Sutras, and constructed images. Among the temples he established were Western Bliss Gardens Monastery, Cixing (Flourishing Compassion) Chan

Monastery, and the Buddhist Lecture Hall. During a period of over ten years, he created extensive Dharma-affinities with the people of Hong Kong. The Sutras he lectured on included the *Earth Store Sutra*, the *Vajra Sutra*, the *Amitabha Sutra*, the *Shurangama Sutra*, and the "Universal Door Chapter" of the *Dharma Flower Sutra*. He held such Dharma assemblies as the Great Compassion Repentance, the Medicine Master Repentance, and recitation and meditation sessions. He published the magazine *Hsin Fa (Mind Dharma)*. As a result of his zealous efforts to propagate the Dharma, Buddhism flourished in Hong Kong. During that time he also visited such countries as Thailand and Burma to study Theravada Buddhism. He hoped to establish communication between the Mahayana and the Theravada traditions and to unite the different sects of Buddhism.

In 1959, the Master saw that conditions were ripe in the West, and he instructed his disciples to establish the Sino-American Buddhist Association (later renamed the Dharma Realm Buddhist Association) in the United States. In 1961 he traveled to Australia and preached the Dharma for one year. Since the conditions were not yet ripe there, he returned to Hong Kong in 1962. Later that year, at the invitation of Buddhists in America, the Master traveled alone to the United States and raised the banner of the Proper Dharma at the Buddhist Lecture Hall in San Francisco. Living in a damp, windowless basement that resembled a grave, he called himself "The Monk in the Grave." When the Cuban Missile Crisis broke out, the Master embarked on a thirty-five-day fast to pray for an end to hostilities and for world peace. By the end of his fast, the crisis had been resolved.

During the Shurangama Study and Practice Summer Session in 1968, over thirty students from the University of Washington in Seattle went to San Francisco to study with the Master. At the end of the session, five of them requested permission to shave their heads and leave the home-life. That was the beginning of the Sangha in the history of American Buddhism. The Master devoted himself to propagating the Dharma, directing the translation of the Buddhist Canon, and developing education. He accepted many disciples, established monasteries, and set forth principles. He exhorted his disciples to work hard in order to cause the Proper Dharma to flourish eternally throughout the Dharma Realm.

The Master lectured on the Sutras and spoke the Dharma every day for several decades, explaining profound principles in a way that made them easy to understand. He also trained his left-home and lay disciples to explain the teachings. He led various delegations to disseminate the Dharma at various universities and in various countries around the world, with the aim of leading beings to turn toward goodness and to discover their innate wisdom.

To date over a hundred volumes of the Master's explanations of the scriptures have been translated into English, and some have also been translated into Spanish, Vietnamese, Japanese, and other languages. The Master's aim is to translate the Buddhist Canon into all the world's languages so that the Dharma will become popular worldwide.

The Master established Instilling Goodness Elementary School, Developing Virtue Secondary School, Dharma Realm Buddhist University, and the Sangha and Laity Training Programs at the City of Ten Thousand Buddhas.

Many of the branch monasteries of Dharma Realm Buddhist Association have classes for children as well. These educational programs are based on the eight virtues of filiality, fraternal respect, loyalty, trustworthiness, propriety, righteousness, incorruptibility, and a sense of shame. In order to encourage students to develop the virtues of kindness, compassion, joy, and charity and to educate them to become men and women of integrity who will be able to contribute to society, the boys and girls study separately and the volunteer teachers regard education as their personal responsibility.

The Master taught his disciples to meditate, recite the Buddha's name, practice repentance, study the Sutras, and observe the precepts strictly. He taught them to eat only one meal a day (at midday) and to always wear the precept sash. He taught them to dwell in harmony and to encourage each other. Under his guidance, a Sangha that practices and maintains the Proper Dharma has grown up in the West. The Master established the City of Ten Thousand Buddhas as an international spiritual community where students and truthseekers can study and work together for the cause of world peace and harmony among religions.

The Master's life was one of total selflessness. He vowed to take the suffering and hardships of all living beings upon himself, and to dedicate to them all the blessings and happiness that he himself ought to enjoy. He practiced what was difficult to practice and endured what was difficult to endure. No amount of hardship could deter him from fulfilling his lofty resolves. He composed a verse expressing his principles:

Freezing, we do not scheme.
Starving, we do not beg.
Dying of poverty, we ask for nothing.
According with conditions, we do not change.
Not changing, we accord with conditions.
We adhere firmly to our three great principles.
We renounce our lives to do the Buddha's work.
We take the responsibility to mold our own destinies.
We rectify our lives as the Saṅgha's work.
Encountering specific matters,
    we understand the principles.
Understanding the principles, we apply
    them in specific matters.
We carry on the single pulse of the patriarchs'
    mind-transmission.

Through his unwavering maintenance of the six guiding principles of not fighting, not being greedy, not seeking, not being selfish, not pursuing personal advantage, and not lying, he brought benefit to many. He dedicated himself to serving others and taught them with wisdom and compassion. His personal example influenced countless people to change their faults and to walk upon the pure, bright path to enlightenment.

Although the Master manifested entry into Nirvana on June 7, 1995 (the tenth day of the fifth lunar month), he constantly turns the infinite Dharma wheel. He came from empty space and returned to empty space without leaving a trace. The least we can do in return for the Master's deep and profound kindness is to carefully follow his teachings, hold to our principles, and advance vigorously toward Bodhi.

The Eighteen Great Vows
of the Venerable Master Hua

1. I vow that as long as there is a single Bodhisattva in the three periods of time throughout the ten directions of the Dharma Realm, to the very end of empty space, who has not accomplished Buddhahood, I too will not attain the right enlightenment.

2. I vow that as long as there is a single Pratyekabuddha in the three periods of time throughout the ten directions of the Dharma Realm, to the very end of empty space, who has not accomplished Buddhahood, I too will not attain the right enlightenment.

3. I vow that as long as there is a single Shravaka in the three periods of time throughout the ten directions of the Dharma Realm, to the very end of empty space, who has not accomplished Buddhahood, I too will not attain the right enlightenment.

4. I vow that as long as there is a single god in the Triple Realm who has not accomplished Buddhahood, I too will not attain the right enlightenment.

5. I vow that as long as there is a single human being in the worlds of the ten directions who has not accomplished Buddhahood, I too will not attain the right enlightenment.

6. I vow that as long as there is a single asura who has not accomplished Buddhahood, I too will not attain the right enlightenment.

7. I vow that as long as there is a single animal who has not accomplished Buddhahood, I too will not attain the right enlightenment.

8. I vow that as long as there is a single hungry ghost who has not accomplished Buddhahood, I too will not attain the right enlightenment.

9. I vow that as long as there is a single hell-dweller who has not accomplished Buddhahood, I too will not attain the right enlightenment.

10. I vow that as long as there is a single god, immortal, human, asura, air-bound or water-bound creature, animate or inanimate object, or a single dragon, beast, ghost, or spirit, and so forth, of the spiritual realm that has taken refuge with me and has not accomplished Buddhahood, I too will not attain the right enlightenment.

11. I vow to fully dedicate all blessings and bliss which I myself ought to receive and enjoy to all living beings of the Dharma Realm.

12. I vow to fully take upon myself all sufferings and hardships of all the living beings in the Dharma Realm.

13. I vow to manifest innumerable bodies as a means to gain access into the minds of living beings throughout the universe who do not believe in the Buddhadharma,

causing them to correct their faults and tend toward wholesomeness, repent of their errors and start anew, take refuge in the Triple Jewel, and ultimately accomplish Buddhahood.

14. I vow that all living beings who see my face or even hear my name will fix their thoughts on Bodhi and quickly accomplish the Buddha Way.

15. I vow to respectfully observe the Buddha's instructions and cultivate the practice of eating only one meal per day.

16. I vow to enlighten all sentient beings, universally responding to the multitude of differing potentials.

17. I vow to obtain the five eyes, six spiritual powers, and the freedom of being able to fly in this very life.

18. I vow that all of my vows will certainly be fulfilled.

Conclusion:

I vow to save the innumerable living beings.
I vow to eradicate the inexhaustible afflictions.
I vow to study the illimitable Dharma-doors.
I vow to accomplish the unsurpassed Buddha Way.

Glossary

This glossary is an aid for readers unfamiliar with the Buddhist vocabulary. Definitions have been kept simple, and are not necessarily complete.

Amitabha Buddha: The Buddha Amitabha is the Buddha of the Western Land of Ultimate Bliss. He is known as Amitabha "infinite light" and Amitayus "infinite life."

Ananda: One of the ten great disciples of the Buddha Shakyamuni, Ananda was the Buddha's first cousin and his attendant. He also compiled and edited the sutras. His name means rejoicing, because he was born on the day the Buddha realized Buddhahood. His father also rejoiced and gave him that name. The entire country celebrated the Buddha's enlightenment on that day. With his flawless memory, Ananda was able to remember all the sutras the Buddha spoke and was foremost among the Buddha's disciples in erudition.

anuttarasamyaksaṁbodhi: This is a Sanskrit term referring to the perfect and universal enlightenment of a Buddha. It is variously translated as meaning "utmost, right and perfect enlightenment"; "supreme, orthodox, and equal awakening"; or the like. This term includes the levels of enlightenment of the Bodhisattva and Arhat within that of the Buddha.

asuras: The category of asuras includes all beings who like to fight. Asuras who use their pugnacious natures beneficially join the armed forces and protect their countries. Asuras who use their propensity to fight in evil ways end up as thieves, robbers, and gunmen. Asuras may live in the heavens, among people, in the animal realm, or as ghosts.

Avalokiteshvara Bodhisattva: One of the four Bodhisattvas of greatest importance in Mahayana Buddhism, Avalokiteshvara is the Bodhisattva of Compassion and the disciple and future successor of the Buddha Amitabha in the Western Land of Ultimate Bliss. His name, which is Sanskrit, is often translated as Observer of the Sounds of the World. It can also be interpreted as meaning Contemplator of Self-Mastery.

Bhagavan (World Honored One): (See Ten Names for the Buddhas)

Bhikshu: Bhikshu is a Sanskrit word; it is the technical designation for a fully ordained Buddhist monk, one who leads a pure and celibate life and who upholds the basic 250 monastic regulations.

Bhikshuni: Bhikshuni is a Sanskrit term that designates a Buddhist nun. It is the feminine form of Bhikshu.

Bodhi: Bodhi is Sanskrit. It means enlightenment, of which there are many levels.

Bodhisattva: Bodhisattva (bodhi = enlightenment + sattva = being) is a Sanskrit word which can be interpreted in two ways: The Bodhisattva is an enlightened one among sentient beings, and he also enlightens sentient beings. A Bodhisattva is someone who has resolved to become a Buddha and who is cultivating the Path to becoming a Buddha.

Brahma Conduct: Brahma conduct means "pure deeds" and refers to anyone who holds the precepts purely.

Brahmans. An externalist way that worshipped fire. See Indian Caste System.

Buddha: Buddha means "awakened" or "enlightened one." It is a title which is applied to those who have reached perfect enlightenment (*anuttarasamyaksambodhi*) and who have perfect wisdom and universal compassion. The Buddha of the present historical period is known as the Buddha Shakyamuni. There were also Buddhas prior to his time; there were and are Buddhas in other worlds; and there will be Buddhas in the future, both in our world and in others.

Condition Enlightened Ones: Same as Those Enlightened to Conditions (see Pratyekabuddhas) .

dhāraṇī: A Sanskrit word, dhāraṇī is interpreted to mean "unite and hold." Dhāraṇī, sometimes called "mantras," unite all dharmas and hold limitless meanings. They are the chief, the head, and the origin of all dharmas. (See Mantra)

Dharma: This is the teachings of the Buddha and is one of the Three Jewels. (See Triple Jewel)

Dharma Door: A Dharma door is an entrance to the Dharma, a teaching about a way or method of practice leading to enlightenment.

Dharma Image Age: (See Three Ages)

Dharma Prince: Buddhas are called Dharma Kings. Dharma Princes are Bodhisattvas, because they are next in line for Buddhahood. Mañjuśrī Bodhisattva is often called the Dharma Prince because he is the senior Bodhisattva.

dragons: Dragons are related to snakes and worms. They have the power to change their size and form, and they are responsible for the changes in weather. (See Eightfold Pantheon and garudas.)

Eightfold Pantheon: Gods, dragons, *yakṣas, gandharvas, asuras, garuḍas, kinnaras,* and *mahoragas* make up eight categories of beings that are not ordinarily visible to the human eye; however, their subtle bodies can be clearly seen by those with higher spiritual powers. Each is discussed under its separate entry.

Eighty Subtle Characteristics: These are the secondary physical attributes of all Buddhas. (See also Thirty-two Features)

Five Rebellious Acts: These are five of the most serious violations of which it is very difficult to repent. They are (1) patricide, (2) matricide, (3) killing an Arhat, (4) spilling the Buddha's blood, and (5) destroying the harmony of the Saṅgha.

flesh-cowl: This is the flesh protuberance on top of the Buddha's head. It is one of the Thirty-two Features of the Buddhas.

Four Continents: The four inhabited continents of every world system. They are situated north, south, east and west of the central mountain Sumeru. In the east is Purva-videha; in the south is Jambu-dvipa; in the west is Apara-godaniya; and in the north is Uttara-kuru.

Four Kinds of Kindness: There are four kinds of kind people to whom living beings owe a debt. They are (1) mothers and fathers, (2) teachers, (3) rulers, and (4) benefactors.

gandharvas: Gandharvas are "incense-inhaling spirits," musicians in the court of the Jade Emperor. When the emperor wants some music, he lights some incense and the gandharvas all come to play music.

Ganges River: The major river in northern India. It is sacred for the Hindus.

garudas: Garudas are great golden-winged birds. They have a wingspan of about 3000 miles. When they flap their wings, the ocean waters part and all the dragons at the bottom of the sea are exposed as potential meals. The dragons have no time to transform into anything. They are gobbled up on the spot by the garudas, who eat them with the same relish as we eat noodles.

gods: Gods, according to Buddhist teaching, live in various heavens. They are not immortal or omnipotent. They do have long life spans and various spiritual powers. Anyone can be reborn as a god by generating the appropriate good karma; however, gods are not enlightened. They eventually die and are reborn in lower realms according to their karma.

Great Vehicle: (See Mahayana)

Hearer: (see Shravaka)

karma. This Sanskrit word means "deeds" or "what is done." Karma can be good, evil, or neutral and is created by the body, mouth, and mind. Seeds of karma are stored in the eighth consciousness and transmigrate with it until the appropriate rewards or retributions are undergone for those deeds done.

karmic hindrances (obstacles): Obstructions or hindrances from past deeds which obstruct one from attaining enlightenment.

King Yama: Lord of the underworld. He is the judge of karma determining where beings are reborn.

kinnaras: *Kinnaras* are another kind of musical spirit (see *gandharvas*) with a single horn on their head. The Jade Emperor does a lot of entertaining and always has them play music in his palace so the gods can dance.

koti: *Koti* is a Sanskrit term meaning one hundred thousand, one million, or ten million.

kṣatriyas: *Kṣatriyas* are the ruling｜martial caste of India. The Buddha's clan, the Shakyas, was a member of the *ksatriyas* caste.

Lion's Roar: The Buddha's voice is called the Lion's Roar because all must listen to him when he speaks.

Mahasattva: Mahasattva is a Sanskrit word meaning "great being." It is the title of a great Bodhisattva.

Mahasthamaprapta Bodhisattva: This Bodhisattva's name translates as "Great Strength," and he is the third of the three Sages of Amitabha Buddha's Pure Land. The others are Amitabha Buddha and Avalokiteshvara Bodhisattva.

Mahayana: Mahayana means "great vehicle" because it teaches its adherents to follow the Path of the Bodhisattva, which leads to Buddhahood. The Bodhisattva is reborn voluntarily in order to aid all living beings to become enlightened. The Mahayana is also called Northern Buddhism because it came to be found in China, Korea, Japan, and Tibet.

mahoragas: *Mahoragas* are huge snake spirits.

Maitreya Bodhisattva: Maitreya, also known as Ajita, is one of the great Bodhisattva-disciples of the Buddha. He is

213

foremost in the perfection of patience, and in a future age he will become the next Buddha.

Mañjuśrī Bodhisattva: Mañjuśrī, a Sanskrit word, is interpreted as "wonderful virtue" or "wonderfully auspicious." Of the Bodhisattvas, Mañjuśrī has the greatest wisdom, and so he is known as "The Greatly Wise Bodhisattva Mañjuśrī." Among the Bodhisattvas, he holds the highest rank

mantra: Mantras are phrases of sound whose primary meaning or meanings are not cognitive, but on a spiritual level that transcends ordinary linguistic understanding.

Nirvana: Nirvana is a Sanskrit term that is interpreted in various ways: (1) cessation, or extinction, referring to the elimination of afflictions at the time of enlightenment or to the ceasing to be of the skandhas when an enlightened person at death chooses to be reborn no longer; (2) freedom from desire; and (3) no longer either coming into being or ceasing to be.

Pratyekabuddha: Pratyekabuddhas are holy sages enlightened to conditions. When there is a Buddha in the world, they are called those "enlightened to conditions." When there is no Buddha in the world, they are called "solitary enlightened ones" because they are able to become enlightened by themselves.

precepts: The precepts are the moral rules laid down by the Buddha for all his disciples to follow. They are described as being as brilliant as vajra. They are the original source of all Buddhas, the original source of all Bodhisattvas, and the seed of the Buddha-nature.

Saha World: The name of the world we live in, which means "can be endured." The suffering in our Saha World is not so severe as to make it unbearable.

Saṅgha: Saṅgha is a Sanskrit word meaning "community" and in Buddhism refers to the monastic community of monks (bhikshus) and nuns (bhikshunis) . They are the transmitters of the tradition and the teachers of the lay community. Fully ordained members of the Saṅgha adhere to a large number of moral precepts, including celibacy, as a guide for their behavior. The Saṅgha is the third of the Three Jewels. (See Triple Jewel)

Sīla: Sīla is a Sanskrit term which means the moral precepts.

Shravaka: Shravaka is Sanskrit and literally means "one who hears or listens." It is traditionally explained as referring to those who "hear the sound of the Buddha's teaching and awaken to the Way." They become enlightened as soon as they hear the Buddha speak the Dharma of the Four Holy Truths, and they are one of the Two Vehicles, the other vehicle being those Enlightened to Conditions. (See also Pratyekabuddhas)

Six Paths: The Six Paths of Rebirth are divided into the three wholesome paths of (1) gods, (2) humans, and (3) *asuras,* and the three (evil) paths of (4) animals, (5) ghosts, and (6) hell-dwellers.

Skill-in-means: Skill-in-means [an alternate translation of "expedient Dharma"] refers to provisional teachings: clever, expedient devices. Skill-in-means can also be explained as meaning "exclusive Dharmas." They are not restrained by any fixed standards; therefore, they are "expedient." In teaching beings, Bodhisattvas devise various kinds of methods according to the situation at hand.

Sutra: Discourse spoken by Buddhas, Bodhisattvas, or other qualified sages.

ten directions: North, south, east, west, northeast, southeast, northwest, southwest, above, and below make up the ten directions.

Ten Names for the Buddhas: Each Buddha may be referred to by ten names which are: (1) Thus Come One (Tathagata), (2) One Worthy of Offerings, (3) Of Proper and Equal Enlightenment, (4) Perfect in Understanding and Practice, (5) Well Gone One, (6) Supreme Lord Who Understands the

World, (7) Regulating Hero, (8) Teacher of Gods and Human, (9) Buddha, (10) World Honored One (Bhagavan).

Ten Wholesome Deeds: The Ten Wholesome Deeds are abstention from (1) killing, (2) stealing, (3) sexual misconduct, (4) duplicity, (5) harsh speech, (6) lying, (7) irresponsible speech, (8) greed, (9) anger, and (10) foolishness.

Thirty-two Features: These are the primary physical characteristics which all Buddhas possess. They are the karmic result of a hundred kalpas of cultivation on the Bodhisattva Path.

Three Ages: The Three Ages are (1) the Orthodox Dharma Age, (2) The Dharma Image/Semblance Age, and (3) the Dharma-Ending Age. The era when the Buddha dwelled in the world was called the Orthodox Dharma Age. At that time the Buddha taught the Dharma, and there were genuine Arhats and great Bodhisattvas; the sages were dwelling in the world. The Orthodox Dharma Age lasted for one thousand years. The Dharma Image Age began after the Buddha entered nirvana. During this period, people who cultivated the Way were few; those who were attached to external appearances were many. People stressed the creation of Buddha-images and many were made, but genuine cultivators were few. During the Dharma Ending Age, the last of the Three Ages of Dharma, the understanding and practice of the Buddhadharma gradually declines and finally disappears.

Three Paths: (See Six Paths)

Three Realms: The Three Realms refers to the realm of desire, the realm of form, and the formless realm. Living beings within the realm of desire still have desire—greed and lust. Living beings within the realm of form do not have such heavy desire; however, they still have a physical form and appearance. They are still attached to appearances, and therefore they are not apart from the marks of self, others, living beings, and life spans. Living beings of the formless

216

realm are without form or shape, yet they still have consciousness, and they are attached to that consciousness.

Thus Come One (Tathagata): (See Ten Names for the Buddhas)

Triple Jewel: The Triple Jewel, also called the Three Jewels or Gems, comprises: (1) the Buddha, (2) the Dharma, and (3) the Saṅgha. They are Buddhism's greatest treasures. For further information, see the individual entries for each.

Upasaka: An Upasaka is a layman. The term Upasaka means "a man who is close in work," working closely with the Triple Jewel.

Upasika: Upasika is the feminine form of Upasaka.

vaiḍūrya: *Vaiḍūrya* is the Sanskrit term for lapis lazuli.

Vaiśālī: An ancient kingdom and city in India north of present-day Patna.

wang liang: A kind of malevolent ghost.

Western Land of Ultimate Bliss: Amitabha Buddha's pure land. By the power of his vows, Amitabha Buddha leads all beings to rebirth in his country, where they realize Buddhahood. This power attracts living beings to the Western Land of Ultimate Bliss, just as a magnet attracts iron filings. If living beings do not attain enlightenment, Amitabha Buddha himself won't realize Buddhahood either.

yakṣa: *Yakṣas* are "speedy ghosts." They get around very fast. There are ground-traveling, space-traveling, and water-traveling yakshas. They are very fierce. Some specialize in sapping people of their energy; some drink human blood; and some eat people's essence. They come in many varieties.

Index

A

afflictions, 45
Akṣobhya, 26
Amitabha Buddha, 26
asaṅkhyeya, 63
Ananda, 40
  asks the Buddha four
    matters, 34
anger, 56
Arhats, 44
asuras, 56
audience, 47

B

Bhagavan
  six meanings of, 43
Bhikshu
  three meanings of, 48
Bhikshus
  evil-natured, 39
birth and death, 70
  of thoughts, 71
  physical, 71
  two kinds of, 71
blindness, 76
Bodhi Way, 69
Bodhisattva, 27, 50
  levels of, 51
  of equal enlightenment, 58

body, 37, 65, 75
Brahmans, 52
Buddha, 28, 32, 45
  three enlightenments of, 51

C

clothing, food, and shelter, 29
compilation of the Sutras, 40
cultivators
  who neglect precepts, 54
cycles of worlds, 56

D

deafness, 76
death, 29
demons from the heavens, 49
desire, 45
deviant paths, 68
Dharma, 41
Dharma body and wisdom, 41
Dharma Master, 52
Dharma Ending Age, 60
Dharma Image Age, 60
Dharma-protecting spirits, 54
Dharma-protectors, 30
  the eightfold division, 57
dharmas, 38

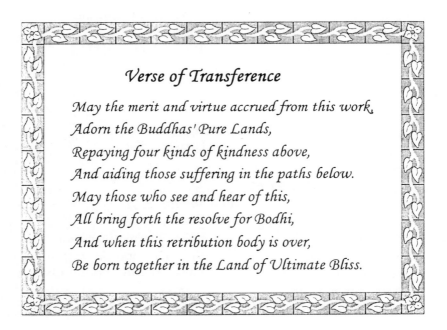

Verse of Transference

May the merit and virtue accrued from this work,
Adorn the Buddhas' Pure Lands,
Repaying four kinds of kindness above,
And aiding those suffering in the paths below.
May those who see and hear of this,
All bring forth the resolve for Bodhi,
And when this retribution body is over,
Be born together in the Land of Ultimate Bliss.

Namo Dharma Protector Wei Tuo Bodhisattva

Buddhist Text Translation Society Publications

Buddhist Text Translation Society
International Translation Institute
1777 Murchison Drive
Burlingame, California 94010-4504 USA
Phone: 650-692-5912   Fax: 650-692-5056

When Buddhism first came to China from India, one of the most important tasks required for its establishment was the translation of the Buddhist scriptures from Sanskrit into Chinese. This work involved a great many people, such as the renowned monk National Master Kumarajiva (fifth century), who led an assembly of over 800 people to work on the translation of the Tripitaka (Buddhist canon) for over a decade. Because of the work of individuals such as these, nearly the entire Buddhist Tripitaka of over a thousand texts exists to the present day in Chinese.

Now the banner of the Buddha's Teachings is being firmly planted in Western soil, and the same translation work is being done from Chinese into English. Since 1970, the Buddhist Text Translation Society (BTTS) has been making a paramount contribution toward this goal. Aware that the Buddhist Tripitaka is a work of such magnitude that its translation could never be entrusted to a single person, the BTTS, emulating the translation assemblies of ancient times, does not publish a work until it has passed through four committees for primary translation, revision, editing, and certification. The leaders of these committees are Bhikshus (monks) and Bhikshunis (nuns) who have devoted their lives to the study and practice of the Buddha's teachings. For this reason, all of the works of the BTTS put an emphasis on what the principles of the Buddha's teachings mean in terms of actual practice and not simply hypothetical conjecture.

The translations of canonical works by the Buddhist Text Translation Society are accompanied by extensive commentaries by the Venerable Tripitaka Master Hsuan Hua and are available in softcover only unless otherwise noted.

Buddhist Sutras

Amitabha Sutra. This Sutra, which was spoken by the Buddha without having been formally requested as other Sutras were, explains the causes and circumstances for rebirth in the Land of Ultimate Bliss of Amitabha (Limitless Light) Buddha. The commentary includes extensive information on common Buddhist terminology and stories about many of the Buddha's foremost disciples. ISBN 0-917512-01-4. 204 pp. $8.00.

> (Explicación General del Sutra en que El Buda Habla de Amitabha. Spanish edition. ISBN 0-917512-30-6. $8.00.)

Dharma Flower (Lotus) Sutra. In this Sutra, which was spoken in the last period of the Buddha's teaching, the Buddha proclaims the ultimate principles of the Dharma, which unite all previous teachings into one. When completed, the translation of the entire Sutra and commentary will comprise an estimated fifteen to twenty volumes. The following are those volumes that have been published to date. Set of ten volumes, $79.50.

> **Volume I. Foreword by Venerable Master Hua.** Discusses the five periods and the eight teachings of the T'ien T'ai School and then analyzes the School's Five Profound Meanings as they relate to the Sutra. The last portion tells of the life of Tripitaka Master Kumarajiva, who translated the Sutra from Sanskrit into Chinese. ISBN 0-917512-16-2. 85 pp.

> **Volume II. Chapter One, Introduction.** Describes the setting for the speaking of the Sutra, the assembly that gathered to hear it, the Buddha's emission of light, the questions asked by Maitreya Bodhisattva, and the response given by Manjushri Bodhisattva. ISBN 0-917512-22-7. 324 pp.

Volume III. Chapter Two, Expedient Methods. After the Buddha emerges from samadhi, he speaks of the vast merit and virtue of the Buddhas. Shariputra beseeches him to expound further on this. After his third request, the Buddha consents and for the first time proclaims that all beings without exception can become Buddhas.
ISBN 0-917512-26-X. 183 pp.

Volume IV. Chapter Three, A Parable. The Buddha explains the purpose of his teachings by means of an analogy of an elder who tries to rescue five hundred children who are absorbed in play in a burning house. ISBN 0-917512-62-6. 371 pp.

Volume V. Chapter Four, Belief and Understanding. Four of the Buddha's foremost Arhat disciples relate a parable about a prodigal son to express their joy upon hearing that they, too, can become Buddhas in the future.
ISBN 0-917512-64-2. 200 pp.

Volume VI. Chapter Five, Medicinal Herbs and Chapter Six, Conferring Predictions. The Buddha uses the analogy of a rain cloud to illustrate how his teaching benefits all beings with total impartiality. He also predicts that the previously mentioned Arhat disciples will become Buddhas in the future. In bestowing his prediction, he tells what their future Buddha names will be and what the names of their world systems and *kalpas* will be, as well as the scope of their Dharma.
ISBN 0-917512-65-0. 161 pp.

Volume VII. Chapter Seven, Parable of the Transformation City. The Buddha teaches that the attainment of his Arhat disciples is like a city that he conjured up as an expedient when they became weary of the journey to Buddhahood. ISBN 0-917512-67-7. 250 pp.

**Volume VIII. Chapter Eight, Five Hundred Disciples Receive Predictions and Chapter Nine, Bestowing Predictions upon

Those Studying and Beyond Study. More than a thousand disciples receive predictions that they will become Buddhas in the future. ISBN 0-917512-71-5. 160 pp.

Volume IX. Chapter Ten, Masters of the Dharma and Chapter Eleven, Vision of the Jewelled Stupa. Chapter Ten explains the vast merit from upholding and propagating the *Wonderful Dharma Lotus Flower Sutra.* In Chapter Eleven, all of the many millions of transformation bodies of Shakyamuni Buddha gather in one place so that those in the assembly can see Many Jewels Buddha, who in the distant past made a vow to appear wherever this Sutra is spoken. ISBN 0-917512-85-5. 270 pp.

Volume X. Chapter Twelve, Devadatta and Chapter Thirteen, Exhortation to Maintain. In Chapter Twelve, the Buddha reveals that Devadatta was once his teacher in a former life, and then bestows a prediction of Buddhahood on him. The eight-year-old dragon girl becomes a Buddha. In Chapter Thirteen, the Buddha bestows predictions of Buddhahood on Bhikshunis. ISBN 0-917512-52-9. 150 pp.

Flower Adornment (Avatamsaka) Sutra. Known as the "King of Kings" of all Buddhist scriptures because of its profundity and great length (81 rolls containing more than 700,000 Chinese characters), this Sutra contains the most complete explanation of the Buddha's state and the Bodhisattva's quest for Awakening. When completed, the entire Sutra text with commentary will comprise from 75 to 100 volumes. The following are those volumes that have been published to date:

Verse Preface. A succinct and eloquent verse commentary by T'ang Dynasty National Master Ch'ing Liang, the Master of seven emperors. The Preface gives a complete explanation of all the fundamental principles contained in the Sutra. This is the first English translation of this text. Bilingual edition, English/Chinese. ISBN 0-917512-28-6. 244 pp. $7.00.

Prologue. A detailed explanation of the principles of the Sutra, by National Master Ch'ing Liang, utilizing the Hsien Shou method of analyzing scriptures known as the Ten Doors. The *Prologue* contains the first Nine Doors. Will be approximately seven to ten volumes upon completion. Set of four books, $38.00. The following volumes have been published to date:

> **First Door. The Causes and Conditions for the Arising of the Teaching** of the *Flower Adornment Sutra*. Complete in one volume. ISBN 0-917512-66-9. 252 pp.

> **Second Door. The Stores and Teachings in Which It Is Contained.** Three volumes as follows:

>> **Part One.** Complete discussion of the Three Stores. Beginning of discussion of the Schools in China. ISBN 0-917512-73-1. 280 pp.

>> **Part Two.** More on Chinese schools. The Indian schools and comparisons between them. ISBN 0-917512-98-7. 220 pp.

>> **Part Three.** Detailed discussion of the Five Hsien Shou Teachings, the sequence of the Teaching Methods, and the inconceivable state of the Flower Adornment. Completes the explanation of the Second Door. ISBN 0-88139-009-7. 160 pp.

The following twenty-two volumes are available as a set only. $174.50.

Flower Store Adorned Sea of Worlds, Chapter Five, Parts One & Two. Describes the universe we live in, including an explanation of principles pertaining to the coming into being of worlds, the wind wheels that uphold them, their orbits, and their mutual attraction. Also, detailed descriptions of the worlds located on the twenty tiers of the lotus that forms the basis of our cosmic structure. ISBN 0-917512-54-5. 250 pp.

Flower Store Adorned Sea of Worlds, Chapter Five, Part Three, and Vairochana, Chapter Six. Conclusion of Chapter Five, "Flower Store Adorned Sea of Worlds," and Chapter Six, "Vairochana," which discusses the causes and conditions of the clear, pure Dharma-body Buddha, Vairochana Buddha. ISBN 0-88139-114-X. 191 pp.

The Names of the Thus Come Ones, Chapter Seven, and The Four Holy Truths, Chapter Eight. In Chapter Seven, the Bodhisattvas gather from the worlds of the ten directions to request that the Buddha speak about the Great Bodhisattva practices, which are explained at great length in later chapters of the *Flower Adornment Sutra*. In Chapter Eight, each of the Four Holy Truths—suffering, accumulation, extinction, and the Way—are explained according to the conditions of ten different worlds plus the Saha World, the world that we inhabit. ISBN 0-88139-014-3. 77 pp.

Bright Enlightenment, Chapter Nine. From the soles of his feet, Shakyamuni Buddha emits light, which continually gets brighter and shines upon more and more different countries in the ten directions. After each time that he emits light, Manjushri Bodhisattva speaks verses praising the virtues of the Buddha. ISBN 0-88139-005-4. 225 pp.

Pure Conduct, Chapter Eleven. This chapter of the Sutra gives a detailed explanation of the pure practices of the Bodhisattva. It is one of the most renowned guides to the Vinaya in the Buddhist canon. ISBN 0-917512-37-5. 255 pp.

Ten Dwellings, Chapter Fifteen. Explains the state of the Ten Dwellings attained by the Bodhisattva. ISBN 0-917512-77-4. 185 pp.

Brahma Conduct, Chapter Sixteen. Explains the meanings of the pure Brahma conduct cultivated by the Bodhisattva. ISBN 0-917512-80-4. 65 pp.

The Merit and Virtue from First Bringing forth the Mind, Chapter Seventeen. Various analogies describe the merit obtained by the Bodhisattva when he first resolves his mind on becoming enlightened. ISBN 0-917512-83-9. 200 pp.

The Ten Inexhaustible Treasuries, Chapter Twenty-two. Explains the Ten Inexhaustible Treasuries attained by the Bodhisattva immediately following the Ten Conducts. ISBN 0-917512-38-3. 184 pp.

Praises in the Tushita Heaven, Chapter Twenty-four. Verses in praise of the Buddha spoken by the great Bodhisattvas after the Buddha arrived in the Tushita Heaven, prior to Vajra Banner Bodhisattva's explanation of the Ten Transferences. ISBN 0-917512-39-1. 130 pp.

Ten Grounds, Chapter Twenty-six, Part One. Contains the First Ground of Happiness, which focuses on the practice of giving. ISBN 0-917512-87-1. 234 pp.

Part Two. Covers the Bodhisattva's Second Ground of Leaving Filth, Third Ground of Emitting Light, and Fourth Ground of Blazing Wisdom. ISBN 0-917512-74-X. 200 pp.

Universal Worthy's Conduct, Chapter Thirty-six. Universal Worthy Bodhisattva explains obstructions that arise from anger; gives methods to correct it when it does arise; and describes the purities, wisdoms, universal entrances, and supremely wondrous minds that result. ISBN 0-88139-011-9. 75 pp.

Entering the Dharma Realm, Chapter Thirty-nine. This chapter, which makes up one quarter of the entire Sutra, contains the spiritual journey of the Youth Good Wealth in his search for Ultimate Awakening. During his quest, he meets fifty-three Good Teachers, each of whom represents a successive stage on the Bodhisattva path. This is the first English translation of this chapter.

Part One. Describes the setting for the Youth's quest and his meeting with Manjushri Bodhisattva. ISBN 0-917512-68-5. 280 pp.

Part Two. In this volume Good Wealth meets his first ten teachers, who represent the positions of the Ten Dwellings. ISBN 0-917512-70-7. 250 pp.

Part Three. In this volume Good Wealth is taught by the ten teachers who correspond to the Ten Conducts. ISBN 0-917512-72-3. 250 pp.

Part Four. In this volume Good Wealth meets the ten teachers who represent the Bodhisattvas of the Ten Transferences. ISBN 0-917512-76-6. 185 pp.

Part Five. In this volume Good Wealth meets the six teachers who represent the first six Grounds. ISBN 0-917512-81-2. 300 pp.

Part Six. Good Wealth meets the teachers on the seventh to tenth Grounds. ISBN 0-917512-48-0. 320 pp.

Part Seven. Uniting with Conditions and Entering the True Mark. Good Wealth visits eleven teachers. ISBN 0-88139-050-X. 156 pp.

Part Eight. The Youth Good Wealth visits his final three teachers, the Bodhisattvas Maitreya, Manjushri, and Universal Worthy. ISBN 0-88139-055-0. 224 pp.

Universal Worthy's Conduct and Vows, Chapter Forty. A detailed explanation of Universal Worthy Bodhisattva's ten great kinds of practice, considered to be the foremost of all practices. ISBN 0-917512-84-7. 300 pp.

Heart Sutra & Verses without a Stand. Considered the most popular Sutra in the world today, the text of the *Heart Sutra* explains the meaning of Prajna-paramita, the perfection of wisdom that is able to clearly perceive the emptiness of all phenomena. Each line in the text is accompanied by an eloquent verse by the Venerable Master Hsuan Hua and his commentary, which contains an explanation of most of the fundamental Buddhist concepts. ISBN 0-917512-27-8. 160 pp. $7.50.

Shurangama Sutra. This Sutra gives the most detailed explanation of the Buddha's teachings concerning the mind. It includes an analysis of where the mind is located, an explanation of the origin of the cosmos, a discussion of the specific workings of *karma*, a description of all the realms of existence, and an exposition on the fifty kinds of deviant samadhi-concentrations, which can delude us in our search for awakening. Also, in this Sutra twenty-five enlightened sages explain the methods they used to become enlightened. Set of first seven volumes $59.50.

> **Volume One.** The Venerable Ananda presents seven ideas on the location of the mind. The Buddha shows how each one is incorrect and then explains the roots of the false and the true. ISBN 0-917512-17-0. 289 pp.

> **Volume Two.** The Buddha explains individual and collective karma, and he reveals the true mind by displaying ten different aspects of the seeing nature.
> ISBN 0-917512-25-1. 212 pp.

> **Volume Three.** The Buddha gives a clear description of the qualities of all the sense fields, their respective consciousnesses, and all the internal and external elemental forces of the universe. He explains how all are ultimately unreal, neither existing through causes nor arising spontaneously. ISBN 0-917512-94-4. 240 pp.

> **Volume Four.** The Buddha talks about the formation of the world, the coming into being of sentient creatures, and the cycle of karmic retribution. ISBN 0-917512-95-2. 200 pp.

Volume Five. Twenty-five sages explain the method each used to transcend the realm of birth and death. Manjushri Bodhisattva selects the method used by the Bodhisattva Kuan Yin of "returning the hearing to listen to the self-nature" as the most appropriate for people in our world system. ISBN 0-917512-96-0. 250 pp.

Volume Six. Includes the Buddha's explanation of the Four Clear and Unalterable Instructions on Purity, how to establish a Bodhimanda, the Shurangama Mantra and its wondrous functions, and the twelve categories of living beings. ISBN 0-917512-97-9. 200 pp.

Volume Seven. Contains an explanation of the fifty-five stages of the Bodhisattva's path to Enlightenment and of how beings fall into the hells and turn in the realms of the ghosts, animals, people, immortals, *asuras,* and the various heavens. ISBN 0-917512-93-6. 270 pp.

Volume Eight. This final volume presents an exposition on fifty deviant mental states associated with the five *skandhas*. In addition to being an invaluable guide for Buddhist practitioners, it offers a framework for the classification of all spiritual experience, both Buddhist and non-Buddhist.
English only, hardcover, ISBN 0-88139-401-7. 453 pp. $20.00.
Bilingual, hardcover, ISBN 0-88139-400-9. 697 pp. $25.00.

Sixth Patriarch Sutra. One of the foremost scriptures of Ch'an Buddhism, this text describes the life and teachings of the remarkable Patriarch of the T'ang Dynasty, Great Master Hui Neng, who, though unable to read or write, was enlightened to the true nature of all things.
Softcover, ISBN 0-917512-19-7. 317 pp. $10.00.
Hardcover, ISBN 0-917512-33-2. 317 pp. $15.00.

Sutra in Forty-two Sections. In this Sutra, which was the first to be transported from India and translated into Chinese, the Buddha gives the most essential instructions for cultivating the Dharma, emphasizing the cardinal virtues of renunciation, contentment, and patience.

First edition, ISBN 0-917512-15-4. 114 pp. $5.00.

Second edition, hardcover, bilingual, ISBN 0-88139-184-0. 347 pp. $12.00.

Sutra of the Past Vows of Earth Store Bodhisattva. This Sutra tells how Earth Store Bodhisattva attained his position among the greatest Bodhisattvas as the Foremost in Vows. It also explains the workings of *karma*, how beings undergo rebirth, and the various kinds of hells. This is the first English translation. Hardcover only, ISBN 0-917512-09-X. 235 pp. $16.00.

English text, without commentary, for recitation also available: ISBN 0-88139-502-1. 120 pp. $7.00

Vajra Prajna Paramita (Diamond) Sutra. One of the most popular scriptures, the *Vajra Sutra* explains how the Bodhisattva relies on the perfection of wisdom to teach and transform beings. ISBN 0-917512-02-2. 192 pp. $8.00.

Commentarial Literature

Buddha Root Farm. A collection of lectures given during an Amitabha Buddha recitation session, explaining the practice and philosophy of the Pure Land School. The instructions are very thorough and especially useful for the beginner. ISBN 0-917512-11-1. 72 pp. $4.00.

City of 10,000 Buddhas Recitation Handbook. Contains all the material covered in the traditional morning, afternoon, and evening services and special services recited daily in Buddhist monasteries in the East and West. Includes scriptures, praises, chants, mantras, repentances, and so forth. Bilingual edition. Chinese/English. ISBN 0-88139-167-0. 240 pp. $7.00.

Filiality: The Human Source. Filiality is the very root of Way virtue. It is the single most vital force that sustains the universe. Therefore, it is only natural that Buddhist disciples base their conduct on an attitude of filial piety and respect for their parents and elders; for the rulers and officials of countries and the world; for the Triple Jewel; and ultimately for all living beings. All beings have at one time or another been our parents. Volumes I and II of this series contain stories from the twenty-four famous tales of filial paragons of China and numerous excerpts from Buddhist Sutras about filial behavior.
Volume One, ISBN 0-88139-006-2, 120 pp. $7.00.
Volume Two, ISBN 0-88139-020-8. 120 pp. $7.00.

Herein Lies the Treasure-trove. Various talks given by the Venerable Master at the City of 10,000 Buddhas.
Volume One, ISBN 0-88139-001-1. 250 pp. $6.50.
Volume Two, ISBN 0-88139-115-8. 150 pp. $6.50.

Listen to Yourself, Think Everything Over. Instructions on how to practice the method of reciting the names of the Buddhas and Bodhisattvas. Also includes a straightforward explanation of how to cultivate Ch'an meditation. All instructions were given during actual meditation and recitation sessions.
Volume One, ISBN 0-917512-24-3. 153 pp. $7.00.
Volume Two, ISBN 0-88139-010-0. 200 pp. $7.00.

Shastra on the Door to Understanding the Hundred Dharmas. A text fundamental to Consciousness Only doctrine, by Vasubandhu Bodhisattva, with commentary by the Venerable Master Hua. Includes lists of the Hundred Dharmas in English, Chinese, and Sanskrit for memorization. ISBN 0-88139-003-8. 130 pp. $6.50.

Song of Enlightenment. The famous lyric poem of the state of the Ch'an sage, by the Venerable Master Yung Chia of the T'ang Dynasty. ISBN 0-88139-100-X. 85 pp. $5.00.

The Ten Dharma Realms Are Not beyond a Single Thought. An eloquent poem on all the realms of being, accompanied by extensive commentarial material and drawings.
ISBN 0-917512-12-X. 72 pp. $4.00.
ISBN 0-88139-503-X. 177 pp. $8.00. Bilingual, English/Chinese

Venerable Master Hua's Talks on Dharma. Collections of talks given by the Venerable Master on various occasions. Emphasis is placed on how to apply Buddhist principles to personal cultivation. Bilingual Chinese/English.
Volume One, ISBN 0-88139-025-9. 227 pp. $7.50.
Volume Two, ISBN 0-88139-026-7. 217 pp. $7.50.
Volume Three, ISBN 0-88139-027-5. 219 pp. $7.50.
Volume Four, ISBN 0-88139-028-3. 217 pp. $7.50.
> (Khai Thị, Quyển 1. Vietnamese translation of Volumes One & Two of *Venerable Master Hua's Talks on Dharma*, complete in one book. ISBN 0-88139-200-6. 264 pp. $10.00.)

Venerable Master Hua's Talks on Dharma during the 1993 Trip to Taiwan. Special Edition of *Talks on Dharma* series. Talks given during the Venerable Master's final visit to Taiwan. Bilingual Chinese/English. Fifteen pages of color photos.
ISBN 0-88139-023-2. 279 pp. $8.50.

Water Mirror Reflecting Heaven. An essay on the fundamental principle of cause and effect, with biographical material on contemporary Buddhist cultivation in China. Clear and to the point; very readable for young and old.
ISBN 0-88139-501-3. 82 pp. $4.00.

Biographical

In Memory of the Venerable Master Hsuan Hua. Compiled following Master Hua's "completion of the stillness" on June 7, 1995, these books contain photos of the Master and the programs he founded as well as biographical accounts of the Master's life, essays, and poems written by the Master's disciples and others whose lives he touched. Volume Two includes photos of the cremation ceremony and other memorial ceremonies. Both volumes are bilingual Chinese/English.
Volume One, softcover, ISBN 0-88139-551-X. 249 pp. $35.00.
Volume One, hardcover, ISBN 0-88139-554-4. 249 pp. $35.00.
Volume Two, hardcover, ISBN 0-88139-553-6. 506 pp. $45.00.
Volume Three, hardcover, ISBN 0-88139-557-9. 447 pp. $40.00.

Pictorial Biography of the Venerable Master Hsü Yün. Prose and verse written by the Venerable Master Hua documenting Venerable Yün's life. Illustrated with brush drawings. Each volume contains 104 sections of prose, verse, and drawings.
Volume One, ISBN 0-88139-008-9. 120 pp.
Volume Two, ISBN 0-88139-116-6. 208 pp.
   Two volume set. $16.00.

Records of High Sanghans. A living tradition is sustained to the extent that it is embodied in its heroes. The Buddhist tradition is enhanced by a large body of literature containing truly moving and inspiring life stories of Sanghans (monastics) who dedicated their bodies and lives to the preservation and propagation of the Sagely Teachings. Volume One covers the life stories of the first eminent Sanghans who brought the Buddhadharma from India to China and the adventures of those first Sanghans who withstood severe trials and hardships as they translated the first Sutras from Indian languages into Chinese.
ISBN 0-88139-012-7. 158 pp. $7.00.

Records of the Life of the Venerable Master Hsüan Hua. The life and teachings of the Venerable Master from his birth in China to the present time in America.

> **Volume One.** Covers the Venerable Master's life in China. ISBN 0-917512-78-2. 96 pp. $5.00.
>> (Spanish edition—Relaciones de la Vida del Maestro Hsuan Hua, Volume 1. ISBN 0-917512-31-6. 69 pp. $8.00.)
>
> **Volume Two.** Covers the events of the Master's life as he cultivated and taught in Hong Kong. Contains many photos, poems, and stories. ISBN 0-917512-10-3. 229 pp. $8.00.

Three Steps, One Bow. The daily journals of American Bhikshus Heng Ju and Heng Yo, who during 1973 and 1974 made a pilgrimage for world peace from Gold Mountain Monastery in San Francisco to Seattle, Washington, making a full prostration (kowtowing) every third step. The pilgrimage was inspired by monks in ancient China who would bow every third step for thousands of miles to a famous monastery or renowned teacher. ISBN 0-917512-18-9. 160 pp. $5.00.

World Peace Gathering. A collection of instructional talks on Buddhism commemorating the successful completion of the bowing pilgrimage of Bhikshus Heng Ju and Heng Yo. ISBN 0-917512-05-7. 128 pp. $5.00.

News from True Cultivators. The letters written by the two more recent "Three Steps, One Bow" monks, Dharma Masters Heng Sure and Heng Ch'au, during their bowing pilgrimage, addressed to the Venerable Abbot and the Assembly of the City of Ten Thousand Buddhas, are uplifting messages to those traversing the path of cultivation and inspiring exhortations to all those concerned with evolving vital and workable methods to alleviate the acute problems of our troubled times. The language is simple; the insights are profound. No one should miss reading these books!
Volume One, ISBN 0-88139-508-0. 130 pp. $6.00.
Volume Two, ISBN 0-88139-024-0. 122 pp. $6.00.

Open Your Eyes, Take a Look at the World. The journals of Bhikshus Heng Sure and Heng Ch'au and Bhikshuni Heng Tao, written during the 1978 Asia-region visit by the Venerable Master and other members of the Sino-American Buddhist Association. ISBN 0-917512-32-4. 347 pp. $9.00.

With One Heart Bowing to the City of 10,000 Buddhas. The moving journals of American Bhikshus Heng Sure and Heng Ch'au, who made a "Three Steps, One Bow" pilgrimage from Gold Wheel Temple in Los Angeles to the City of 10,000 Buddhas, located 110 miles north of San Francisco, from May 1977 to October 1979. Set $63.00.

Volume One. May 6–June 30, 1977.
ISBN 0-917512-21-9. 180 pp.
Volume Two. July 1–October 30, 1977.
ISBN 0-917512-23-5. 322 pp.
Volume Three. October 30–December 20, 1977.
ISBN 0-917512-89-8. 154 pp.
Volume Four. December 17, 1977–January 21, 1978.
ISBN 0-917512-90-1. 136 pp.
Volume Five. January 28–February 18, 1978.
ISBN 0-917512-91-X. 127 pp.
Volume Six. February 19–April 2, 1978.
ISBN 0-917512-92-8. 200 pp.
Volume Seven. April 3–May 24, 1978.
ISBN 0-917512-99-5. 160 pp.
Volume Eight. May 24-September, 1978
ISBN 0-917512-53-7. 232 pp.
Volume Nine. September–October, 1978.
ISBN 0-88139-509-9. 232 pp.

Children's Books

Cherishing Life. Contains verses and brush drawings about not taking life, and public records about cause and effect, drawn from events recorded by Dharma Masters, giving people's awareness of the reasons for their retributions in the animal realm. For elementary age children as well as adults.
Volume One, ISBN 0-88139-004-6. 150 pp. $7.00.
Volume Two, ISBN 0-88139-015-1. 150 pp. $7.00.

Human Roots: Buddhist Stories for Young Readers. Volume One has a total of fourteen stories from the Buddhist canon and historical records. ISBN 0-88139-500-5. 95 pp. $5.00.
Volume Two, ISBN 0-88139-017-8. 138 pp. $5.00.

Music, Novels, & Brochures

Songs for Awakening. Lyrics and guitar music for over forty modern American Buddhist songs. Indexed according to title and first line. With drawings, woodcuts, and photographs. The 9" by 12" songbook makes a fine gift to introduce your friends to Buddhism. ISBN 0-917512-63-4. 112 pp. $8.00.

Awakening. A 12" stereo record album of ten Buddhist songs in Western style (all in English) ranging from pop and rock, to folk and country. Subjects covered include: Bodhisattva vows, the *I Ching*, Ch'an meditation, Lao-Tzu, the *Lotus Sutra*, Abhidharma meditation, and Amitabha Buddha and his Pure Land. $7.00 plus $1.00 shipping in the U.S.A. and $2.00 for international orders.

The Three Cart Patriarch. A 12" stereo lp recorded by and for children, based on the *Monkey Tales* of China. Featuring stories, six musical productions, and many special effects. $7.00 plus $1.00 shipping in the U.S.A. and $2.00 for international orders.

City of 10,000 Buddhas Color Brochure. Over thirty color photos of the scenic center for World Buddhism, along with many poems and a description of the City's activities. 24 pp. $2.00.

Celebrisi's Journey. A novel by David Rounds describing the events in a modern American's quest for enlightenment. (First edition) ISBN 0-917512-14-6. 178 pp. $4.00.

Heng Ch'au's Journal. An account of the remarkable experiences and changes undergone by Bhikshu Heng Ch'au when he first came in contact with Gold Mountain Monastery. ISBN 0-88139-052-6. 20 pp. $1.95.

Ordering Information

Postage & Handling:
The following rates for postage and handling apply to orders of six or fewer books. Up to six audio tapes count as one book. On orders of more than six books, we suggest that purchasers submit their orders for a precise quote on postage and handling costs.

United States: $2.00 for the first book and $0.75 for each additional book. All publications are sent via special fourth class. Allow from two weeks to one month for delivery.

International: $2.50 for the first book and $1.50 for each additional book. All publications are sent via "book rate" or direct mail sack (surface). For countries in which parcels may be lost, we suggest orders be sent via registered mail for an additional $3.25 per parcel of ten books each. We are not responsible for parcels lost in the mail. Allow two to three months for delivery.

■ California residents add 8.25% tax.
■ Make checks payable to: D.R.B.A.

All orders require prepayment, including postage and handling fees, before they will be shipped to the buyer. Submit order to:

Buddhist Text Translation Society
Sagely City of Ten Thousand Buddhas
P.O. Box 217, Talmage, CA 95481-0217 USA
Phone: (707) 462-0939; Fax: (707) 462-0949

or to:

Buddhist Text Translation Society
International Translation Institute
1777 Murchison Drive, Burlingame, CA 94010-4504 USA
Phone: (650) 692-5912; Fax: (650) 692-5056

Most branches of the Dharma Realm Buddhist Association, as well as some retail booksellers, also offer Buddhist Text Translation Society publications for sale.

The Buddhist Monthly—Vajra Bodhi Sea

The Buddhist Monthly—Vajra Bodhi Sea is a monthly journal of orthodox Buddhism which has been published by the Dharma Realm Buddhist Association, formerly known as the Sino-American Buddhist Association, since 1970. Each issue contains the most recent translations of the Buddhist canon by the Buddhist Text Translation Society. Also included in each issue are a biography of a great Patriarch of Buddhism from the ancient past, sketches of the lives of contemporary monastics and lay-followers around the world, articles on practice, and other material. The journal is bilingual, Chinese and English, 48 pages in an 8½" by 11" format.

Single issue $4.00
One year subscription $40.00
Three years $100.00

ISSN 0507-6986 (Postage is included in the subscription fee.)

Send orders to:

> **Vajra Bodhi Sea subscriptions**
> 800 Sacramento Street
> San Francisco, CA 94108
> (415) 421-6117   Fax: (415) 788-6001

Dharma Realm Buddhist Association Branches
Home Page: http:\\www.drba.org
Main Branch:
The City of Ten Thousand Buddhas
P.O. Box 217, Talmage, CA 95481-0217 USA
Tel: (707) 462-0939   Fax: (707) 462-0949

The City of the Dharma Realm
1029 West Capitol Avenue, West Sacramento, CA 95691 USA
Tel: (916) 374-8268

The International Translation Institute
1777 Murchison Drive, Burlingame, CA 94010-4504 USA
Tel: (650) 692-5912   Fax: (650) 692-5056

Institute for World Religions (Berkeley Buddhist Monastery)
2304 McKinley Avenue, Berkeley, CA 94703 USA
Tel: (510) 848-3440   Fax: (510) 548-4551

Gold Mountain Monastery
800 Sacramento Street, San Francisco, CA 94108 USA
Tel: (415) 421-6117   Fax: (415) 788-6001

Gold Sage Monastery
11455 Clayton Road, San Jose, CA 95127 USA
Tel: (408) 923-7243   Fax: (408) 923-1064

Gold Summit Monastery
233-1st Avenue, West Seattle, WA 98119 USA
Tel: (206) 217-9320

Gold Wheel Monastery
235 North Avenue 58, Los Angeles, CA 90042 USA
Tel: (213) 258-6668

Blessings, Prosperity, & Longevity Monastery
4140 Long Beach Boulevard, Long Beach, CA 90807 USA
Tel: (562) 595-4966

Long Beach Monastery
3361 East Ocean Boulevard, Long Beach, CA 90803 USA
Tel: (562) 438-8902

Avatamsaka Hermitage
11721 Beall Mountain Road, Potomac, MD 20854-1128 USA
Tel: (301) 299-3693

Avatamsaka Monastery
1009-4th Avenue, S.W. Calgary, AB T2P 0K8 Canada
Tel: (403) 269-2960

Gold Buddha Monastery
301 East Hastings Street, Vancouver, BC V6A 1P3 Canada
Tel: (604) 684-3754

Dharma Realm Buddhist Books Distribution Society
11th Floor, 85 Chung-hsiao E. Road, Sec. 6, Taipei, R.O.C.
Tel: (02) 786-3022

Tze Yun Tung Temple
Batu 5½, Jalan Sungai Besi, Salak Selatan
57100 Kuala Lumpur, Malaysia
Tel: (03) 782-6560 Fax: (03) 780-1272

Buddhist Lecture Hall
31 Wong Nei Chong Road, Top Floor
Happy Valley, Hong Kong
Tel: 2572-7644